ARCHIBALD MacLEISH

by SIGNI LENEA FALK
Coe College

 93

Twayne Publishers, Inc. :: New York

To C. C. T.

MANUFACTURED IN THE UNITED STATES OF AMERICA BY
UNITED PRINTING SERVICES, INC.
NEW HAVEN, CONN.

Preface

ARCHIBALD MacLEISH has lived close to his own time. The half century between 1911 and 1961 has brought more revolutionary changes in the political, scientific, and social world than any other fifty years in history—and there have also been major changes in poetry. The present study is concerned with the poetry, drama, and prose of Archibald MacLeish produced in this revolutionary half century and with his public life as it impinges on his writing. It is an attempt to suggest the range and variety of his poetry, the evolution of his own theory of poetry and of poetic drama, and the development of his conviction about the role of the poet in modern society.

MacLeish represents the point of view that grants to poetry the experiences not only of the private but also of the public world; and his poems exemplify his thesis. Although he learned much about metrics and language during his early years in France, he early rejected the mirror-gazing tendency of the 1920's. He believes that poetry has been better served by men of affairs like Chaucer, Dante, Shakespeare, Milton, and by Chinese poets and generals like Lu Chi and Tu Fu. He believes that the good poet, as the true revolutionary, crystallizes the essential quality of his time and creates the metaphor by which other men live.

With the exception of military service during World War I and residence in France between 1923 and 1928 when he was learning the craft of poetry, he has spent his life in the United States. The Paris years seem to have given him a perspective on the potentiality of American democracy, and his years of public service during the 1940's a deepened insight not only into the misuse of this rare gift of individual freedom but also into the indifference that prevails among the American people. He has spoken out fearlessly; and, despite ridicule and parody, he has persisted in expressing in both verse and polemical essay the need of Americans to revitalize the principle of individual liberty. Throughout his years of public service and of writing directed to a larger public, he has continued to write the subtly designed personal lyrics that established his position as a major American poet.

This study has been organized chronologically for a number of reasons. Certain poems belong to certain periods, as do certain plays, certain speeches, certain essays. The significance of many of these pieces relates to specific events or conditions. MacLeish experimented in several poetic forms popular at different periods in these last five decades and has achieved for himself various patterns of lyric stanza and line. As a practicing poet deeply involved at times in public life, he has developed a theory of poetry that rejects the isolation of an "ivory tower" and insists that poetry concern itself with all of life. In recent years he has repeatedly affirmed that these revolutionary decades demand new, positive voices in poetry. The chronological approach also gives a perspective to the critical appraisals: some critics have been somewhat dogmatic in their preferences, or too subjective in their evaluation, or dedicated to a single-minded theory of poetry.

Any critical study of a writer that makes use of fragments of poems and excerpted quotations from his prose must in all decency include an apology to the author. In so short a study as this, in order to give some idea of the scope of the work accomplished in fifty years, it has seemed necessary to quote in fragments. For this, apologies are due the poet. I want to thank Mary B. Hawley and Clyde C. Tull for their careful reading of the manuscript and for their many discerning suggestions.

SIGNI LENEA FALK

Coe College

Acknowledgments

To Archibald MacLeish for permission to quote from his many works in poetry and prose.

To Houghton Mifflin for permission to quote from *Collected Poems 1917-1952, A Time to Speak, A Time to Act,* and *J. B.*

To Gay Wilson Allen for permission to quote from a review in the New York *Times,* January 8, 1961.

To Richard Eberhart for permission to quote from two reviews in the New York *Times,* November 23, 1952 and October 10, 1954.

To Dudley Fitts for permission to quote from a review in the New York *Times,* March 23, 1958.

To Maurice Firuski for permission to quote from *Nobodaddy* by Archibald MacLeish.

To *Fortune* Magazine ("Courtesy of *Fortune* Magazine") to quote from three articles by Archibald MacLeish: March, 1930; July, 1930; December, 1935.

To Harcourt, Brace and World, Inc., for permission to quote from *Land of the Free* by Archibald MacLeish.

To Harper and Row for permission to quote from *The Spiritual Aspects of the New Poetry* by Amos Wilder.

To *Harper's Magazine* for permission to quote from an article by Archibald MacLeish, October, 1959.

To Harvard University Press for permission to quote from *This Music Crept by Me upon the Waters* by Archibald MacLeish.

To *The Nation* for permission to quote from an article by Archibald MacLeish, May 18, 1940, and two reviews, one by Lewis Galantiére, April 17, 1929, and one by Eda Lou Walton, January 10, 1934.

To *The New Republic* for permission to quote from two articles by Archibald MacLeish, December 21, 1932, and July 13, 1953; and a review by Kimon Friar, December 15, 1952.

To the New York *Times* ("Copyright by the New York *Times.* Reprinted by permission.") for permission to quote from articles and reviews which appeared as follows:

Speech by Archibald MacLeish reported in the New York *Times,* May 24, 1940.

Review by Gay Wilson Allen, January 8, 1961.

Reviews by Richard Eberhart, November 23, 1952, and October 10, 1954.

Review by Dudley Fitts, March 23, 1958.

Reviews by Charles Poore, February 4, 1934, and November 29, 1952.

To Princeton University Press for permission to quote from *Fearful Symmetry* by Northrop Frye, 1947.

To the University of Illinois Press, Urbana, for permission to quote from *Poetry and Opinion* by Archibald MacLeish.

Contents

Chronology

1892   Archibald MacLeish born May 7 in Glencoe, Illinois. Father: Andrew MacLeish; mother: Martha Hillard MacLeish.

1907- Hotchkiss School.
1911

1915   A. B., Yale University.

1916   Married Ada Hitchcock, June 21. Children: Kenneth, Brewster Hitchcock (deceased), Mary Hillard, William Hitchcock.

1917   *Tower of Ivory;* with Foreword by Lawrence Mason.

1917- Rose from private to captain, United States Army, France.
1918

1919   LL. B., Harvard University; taught at Harvard: Constitutional Law, International Law.

1920   Admitted to the Massachusetts Bar.

1920- Practiced law in Boston.
1923

1923- With wife and two children went to France to work on poetry; within these years made a five-month trip to Persia.
1928

1924   *The Happy Marriage.*

1925   *The Pot of Earth.*

1926   *Nobodaddy.*

1926   *Streets in the Moon.*

1928   Returned to America to farm at Conway, Massachusetts.

1928   *The Hamlet of A. MacLeish.*

1928- Made trip to Mexico on foot and muleback, following route of Cortés.
1929

1929   John Reed Memorial Prize awarded by *Poetry* Magazine.

1930   *New Found Land.*

1930- Editorial Board, *Fortune* Magazine.
1938

1932   *Conquistador;* awarded Pulitzer Prize; M. A. (honorary), Tufts College.

1933   *Poems 1924-1933. Frescoes for Mr. Rockefeller's City.* Elected, National Institute of Arts and Letters.

1934   *Union Pacific.*

1935   *Panic.*

1936   *Public Speech.*

1937   Guest Professor at Princeton (February).

1937   *The Fall of the City.*

1938-   First Curator of Nieman Foundation of Journalism at
1939   Harvard. Litt. D. from Colby College and from Wesleyan University. *Air Raid. Land of the Free.*

1939-   Librarian of Congress.
1944

1939   Litt. D., Yale University. *America was Promises.*

1940   *The Irresponsibles.* LL. D., Dartmouth College; elected trustee, Museum of Modern Art.

1941-   Director, Office of Facts and Figures.
1942

1941   LL. D., Johns Hopkins University; D. C. L., Union College; L. H. D., University of Pennsylvania; Levinson Prize awarded by *Poetry* Magazine; *The American Cause; A Time to Speak.*

1942   Rede Lecturer, Cambridge University; *American Opinion and the War* (Rede Lecture). *A Time to Act.* D. H. L., Williams College; admitted to the United States Supreme Court Bar; appointed Assistant Director Office War Information.

1943   LL. D., University of California.

1944   American Delegation, Conference of Allied Ministers of Education, London; *American Story.*

1944-   Assistant Secretary of State.
1945

1945   Chairman, United States Delegation, London Conference of United Nations to found United Nations Educational Scientific and Cultural Organization (UNESCO).

1946   Chairman, American Delegation, First General Conference, UNESCO, Paris; American Member, Executive Council, UNESCO; Decorated Commander Legion of Honor (France); elected, American Academy of Arts and Letters; Litt. D., University of Illinois.

1947   Awarded Encomienda Order el Sol del Peru.

1948   *Actfive.* LL. D., Queens University, Ontario; Litt. D., Washington University.

1949-   Boylston Professor of Rhetoric and Oratory at Harvard.
1962

1950   *Poetry and Opinion.*

1951   *Freedom is the Right to Choose.*

1952   *Collected Poems 1917-1952. Trojan Horse.*

1953   Awarded Pulitzer Prize for Poetry; Bollingen Prize for Poetry; Shelley Memorial Award; National Book Award in Poetry; *This Music Crept by Me Upon the Waters.*

1953-   President, American Academy of Arts and Letters.
1956

1954   *Songs for Eve.* Litt. D., Columbia University.

1955   Litt. D., Harvard University.

1956   LL. D., Carleton College.

1958   *J. B.* Antoinette Perry Award in Drama.

1959   Awarded Pulitzer Prize in Drama.

1961   *Poetry and Experience.*

1963   Named Simpson Lecturer at Amherst College.

CHAPTER *1*

The New Poetry

I

THROUGH the first decade of the twentieth century most
English and American poetry was wearing itself thin in
imitation of late nineteenth-century Romanticism. The term
"new poetry" appeared with the anthology, *Des Imagistes*, edited
by Ezra Pound in 1914. By the mid-1920's a poetry emerged
very different from that of the years before World War I;
sometimes it is called "new," sometimes "modern," the terms
vary. This poetry is usually marked by certain qualities: it is
of interest to a limited rather than a general audience; it is a
"difficult," cerebral kind of poetry; it is oblique, characterized
by a private kind of reference; it has certain characteristics
of the nineteenth-century French poetry with its attention to
myth, symbol, and to free association of imagery rather than
to a logical sequence; it is free of conventionally poetic
language and techniques.

Archibald MacLeish has frequently referred to the revolutionary movement in poetry as effected by three men, William
Butler Yeats, Ezra Pound, and T. S. Eliot. Whether or not so
intended, their poetry, he wrote, was a revolt against the
neurotic nineteenth-century idea of poetry. He felt that the
major significance of their verse was the significance of language
—"the recovery of the use of living tongues." The consequence
of this revolution was to return poetry to the public world and
poets to positions of common responsibility.

He felt, however, that none of these three men went far
enough. Pound he called a dismantler, a wrecker of all that was
obsolescent. Eliot was even more destructive than Pound in
the way he broke down "poetic" conventions in imagery, in
sound, and in word associations. Yeats only briefly made of
poetry the public speech of which he was capable. The poetry
of these masters was the "needed and cleansing poetry of literary
revolt," but it belongs to the past: "Revolutionists are rarely
successful builders of the worlds they have brought down. . . .

The responsible language of acceptance and belief is not possible to the poetry of literary revolt."[1]

Archibald MacLeish began writing poetry reminiscent of the late nineteenth century, spent his life forging lyric patterns suitable for his particular poetic expression, and succeeded in becoming a master craftsman in several forms. He also hammered out a theory of poetry for our own time, as well as a conviction of the position of the poet in modern society. The role that he ascribes to the poet goes beyond that of the three masters who were responsible for returning significance to poetry.

II

The significance of the poetic revolution accomplished by the work of Ezra Pound, William Butler Yeats, and T. S. Eliot can be suggested by a brief review of their work. "Poet-pedagogue" Ezra Pound (1885-   ) left the United States in 1908 for a busy, fruitful literary life in London, Paris, and Rapallo. From the philosopher T. E. Hulme, he had developed an interest in the concise forms of the Japanese *hokku*, a verse pattern which in turn led to the Imagist movement. His friendship with Yeats and his translations of Chinese poems and Noh plays had considerable influence on Yeats's *Four Plays for Dancers*. As the European editor of *Poetry*, Pound "discovered" Eliot, and introduced to America both Robert Frost and W. B. Yeats. He was the first to recognize the genius of Rabindranath Tagore and was responsible for the publication of James Joyce's *Portrait of an Artist as a Young Man* (1916) and *Ulysses* (1922).

Eliot says that Pound was the greatest influence on English and American poetry between 1910 and 1922, that he did not create poets, but that he created a situation in which there was a "modern movement in poetry." Pound is a man of great energy and strong opinions, of great affections and insane hatreds. He has been an editor and a teacher. He awakened his poet-colleagues to the study of French poetry—Baudelaire, Rimbaud, Verlaine, Valéry, Laforgue—and to the study of Classical as well as Elizabethan literature. He deeply involved them as well as himself in studies of several languages, of sculpture, and of music. He set up severe standards for writing poetry that involved a disciplined attention to word and meter.

Pound advocated a careful study not only of metrics but of good prose. Eliot once wrote that Ezra Pound's "Art of Poetry" was the only contemporary writing that a poet could study with profit. Pound was original in insisting that poetry was an art that demands "the most arduous application and study." His own poetry, exemplifying theories he expounded, bridges the gap between Swinburne and Browning on the one side and modern poetry on the other. Though his work is at times stiff with his tremendous erudition, at other times it has a Classic simplicity and precision. He believed that the past was intensely richer than the present, and he was interested in literary techniques that would enable a poet to re-create the past. He related the curse of our time, what he called "usura," a worship of money, to a decline of the arts. It was this obsession that perhaps contributed most to his joining the Italian fascists.

MacLeish during his years in Paris came under the influence of Ezra Pound. The startling difference between the insular literary background which MacLeish acquired as an under-graduate at Yale and the introduction to a wide European culture that he received after World War I can be suggested by the extraordinary variety of Ezra Pound's own work. *Personae* (1909)—"personae" are masks which the poet assumes for dramatic dialogues—and *Exultations* (1909) recall unusual cadences which have been credited to the Provençal poets, to Villon, and somewhat to Yeats. *The Cantos* (1925-55), representing a range in style from the discursive to the elliptical, and seemingly confused and disconnected, seems to have a complex structure like that of *The Divine Comedy*. This major work represents not only Pound's interest in Homer, Virgil, and Ovid, as well as Dante, but also his knowledge of Western and Oriental history. Among the earlier translations are the Anglo-Saxon poem, "The Sea Farer," (1912), and the Chinese *Cathay* (1915). Later work includes the Confucian books (1947-50) and the Classical anthology (1954). It is generally agreed that Pound's influence is immeasurable and perhaps more significant than his poetry. It has frequently been noted that Pound and Eliot founded a school of poetry which depends on literary quotation and reference.

MacLeish also learned about poetry from T. S. Eliot, a man whose temperament and training, however, were far different from his own. About 1909 Eliot (1888-1965) began as an esoteric poet to the few, but he emerged a half-century later as a widely recognized symbol for modern poetry. The son of a distinguished family of writers and educators and a student at Harvard, the

Sorbonne, and Oxford, he earned a doctor's degree in philosophy. Finding America a cultural wasteland, about 1915 he left for England which became his adopted country in 1927. He came under the influence of Ezra Pound. Eliot's devotion to the heroic past over the "sterile present" derived from the study of Elizabethan drama, of Donne and other metaphysical poets, and of Dante. His technical tutelage and his lessons in symbolism are said to have come from the French poets. The influence of Pound is readily apparent in his sympathy for literary and religious traditions of the past, in his liking for obscure allusions, and in his habit of drawing parallels between the archetype and the contemporary. On the other hand, Eliot has been fascinated with psychological, anthropological, literary, and religious symbols as Pound has not.

Four of the earlier poems of Eliot seem to have deeply impressed MacLeish during the 1920's, for there are echoes of all four in his own poems, particularly those written during his sojourn in France. Eliot's "The Love Song of J. Alfred Prufrock" and "Gerontian" belong to the earlier derivative period (1909-17) and are characterized by "personal and ironical analysis." *The Waste Land* (1922), reduced by Ezra Pound from "a sprawling manuscript" to the most influential poem of its time, belongs to the tradition of Gray's "Elegy," a graveyard poem redolent of scholarship and much rewriting. The lines of varied melodic pattern and the prevailing tone of despair and decadence reflect Eliot's reading of Baudelaire, Rimbaud, Mallarmé, and Laforgue. But there are other echoes, according to scholars, of Carl Sandburg, of Wallace Stevens, of Ezra Pound, and of T. E. Hulme. The fourth poem, *The Hollow Men* (1925) contrasts the synthetic modern man with the savage primitive; it "pronounced anathema upon a soulless generation."

MacLeish, in later years, differed radically from Eliot's critical approach to literature. Essays in *The Sacred Wood* (1920) began Eliot's attempt to establish a standard of criticism on purely intellectual grounds as more trustworthy than either impressionistic or abstract criticism. Eliot's despairing self-scrutiny led him in the Preface to the essays, *For Launcelot Andrewes* (1928), to disclose what had been implicit in his work all along; he declared himself to be "an Anglo-Catholic in religion, a classicist in literature, and a royalist in politics." Whereas MacLeish also went through a phase of despair, he did not turn his back on the present, as did Eliot, to seek refuge in medieval thought. In *Ash Wednesday* (1930) and in *Murder in the Cathedral* (1935) Eliot advanced "progressively backwards" into the medieval ages and conventional morality. *The Four Quartets* (1943) are four meditations on religious and philosophical subjects, each one named, according to the medieval humors—fire, earth, water, air—and each one, a reflection dealing with an aspect of Christian experience.

Eliot, at first strongly influenced by the French Symbolists, by Pound and the Imagist group, wrote free verse in vivid and concrete images, and in snatches of conversation; he later developed a very individual and distinctive style. In keeping with his identification with the aristocrat, the educated, and the talented, he always, like Pound, speaks to a limited, erudite audience. MacLeish, on the other hand, did not write particularly for the scholar. Both Eliot and Yeats, interested in poetry as a vehicle for ideas, used symbols as a means of dealing with abstractions. This fact alone most clearly distinguishes "modern" from earlier Romantic poetry.

The oldest of the three "revolutionary" poets, William Butler Yeats (1865-1939), Irish poet, dramatist, scholar and critic, is generally recognized as one of the major literary figures of the twentieth century. He not only explored a number of unpopular beliefs such as Rosicrucianism, spiritualism, and magic, but also studied history and anthropology; in addition, he became deeply involved in the main concerns of his time. His life represents the struggle of a poet to maintain his position in a world of science and materialism, to give voice and meaning to the world of the spirit, to distinguish the real from the ideal, the world from the imagination. From the beginning Yeats aimed to give "richness, elegance, magnificence" to the symbols which characterized the age in which he lived. He is representative of the periods in which he worked, ranging from the poetry which was a reflection of the Pre-Raphaelite group of his youth to the highly involved and subtle expression of contemporary experience stated in terms of archetypal myths and private symbols. He is a somewhat unusual literary figure in that he did his best work between the ages of fifty and seventy-five, the result of long dedication to his craft.

MacLeish, like Yeats, began writing poetry that imitated the late nineteenth-century Romantic tradition, and both men went through a literary phase in which they dedicated themselves to the art-for-art's-sake tenet. Both men deepened their poetic education through extensive literary friendships and through wide reading in the literatures of both Western and Oriental cultures. Both men turned to poetic drama and not only learned from the experience but reached a wider audience. Out of his personal and political ties and out of his intuitive understanding of his own people, Yeats wrote a number of plays; between 1903 and 1907 he published several volumes of *Plays for an Irish Theatre.*

The years between 1909 and 1914 mark a change in Yeats's life and art. A number of reasons have been given—Synge's death, bitterness over the course of Irish politics, friendship with Ezra Pound, a renewed study of metaphysical poetry. *The Green Helmet* (1912) and *Responsibilities* (1914) represent the poet who had mastered his craft, an imagination toughened by intellect, verse that had been made harder, more severe, more passionate. In this period Yeats assumed a kind of mask, an anti-self. The latter volume includes poems, topical in some cases, but significant for their incisive observation upon these years. These poems have the quality of public speech and have been particularly admired by MacLeish who wished that Yeats had continued in this vein.

In the twenty-five years that followed the publication of *Responsibilities,* Yeats turned away from the current scene and involved himself deeply in special doctrines and a metaphysical system, in magic and spiritualism. He was often like a man looking for material to write about, and the influence of his wife who helped in that search makes a curious chapter in literary history. The volume of poems, *The Tower* (1929), the work of a sick man, represents Yeats in all his moods and vacillations—his interest in politics, philosophy, friendship, and love. Included are some of his best known poems and some of the best in modern poetry: "Sailing to Byzantium," "The Second Coming," "Leda and the Swan," and "Among School Children." Had Yeats ceased to write at forty, he would have been known as a minor literary figure. With the later years came not only some of his best writing but also honors and recognition, among them the Nobel Prize for 1923.

III

Ezra Pound and T. S. Eliot left their American homes and became permanent expatriates. Archibald MacLeish spent five years in France, learned much about the craft of poetry, and returned to the United States to develop with the years a deeper appreciation of the possibilities of the experiment in democracy and of the eroding forces that prevent its fulfillment. Not only his writing but his life—his fearless commitment to freedom of the mind and to civil liberties—have exemplified what it is to be a thinking and responsible American.

Although the life and work of William Butler Yeats differ in many respects from that of Archibald MacLeish, the two men have much in common: both lives have been dedicated to poetry and scholarship; both have been deeply concerned about the place of the imagination in a world increasingly dedicated to science; both became involved in the political movements of their time; both gained a sharpened sense of language from writing for the theater; both moved from poetry's "ivory tower" to the market place, and gained from the experience; both fearlessly expressed opinions not currently popular; both represent, to a certain degree, the different periods in which they lived and worked. Yeats briefly crystallized the sickness that was destroying Ireland. MacLeish has repeatedly warned Americans about the forces of the extreme right which threaten to destroy a democratic government. And also, like his predecessor, MacLeish with the years has recognized that the great tradition in poetry, in both Western and Oriental cultures, has been strongly masculine and deeply involved in its own time.

The heritage of Archibald MacLeish goes deep into the best of the American tradition. His maternal great-grandfather, Captain Moses Hillard, piloted the *Oneida* across the Atlantic during the early 1800's. His great-grandson, describing the variety of his tasks and responsibilities, his adventures, and the high regard he seems to have enjoyed, suggests that he did not fit the image of the frustrated Puritan invented by the literary historians. It was this grandfather who brought to New York, months after it happened, the story of Napoleon's retreat from Moscow, a story that "loomed in the New York newspapers of the next morning like news of Troy, which, in a sense, it was."[2]

Archibald MacLeish's father was a Scotsman from Glasgow, Andrew MacLeish, one of the early settlers in Chicago, a merchant prince and philanthropist for whom two distinguished service professorships are named at the University of Chicago. His mother, Martha Hillard MacLeish, the third wife of Andrew, and the daughter of a Connecticut Congregational minister, a graduate of Vassar and for a time an instructor there, was president of Rockford College (Illinois) from 1884 to 1888.

Archibald MacLeish was born in 1892 at Glencoe, Illinois. The MacLeish home on Lake Michigan afforded to the sensitive boy many of the nature images that were to appear in his poems. After prep school at Hotchkiss, he went to Yale where his college career was a foreshadowing of a busy life and varied interests. He was not only an athlete but a good student as well, earning election to Phi Beta Kappa in his junior year. He was deeply involved in the literary activities of his college generation, his first poem appearing in the October, 1911, issue of the *Yale Literary Magazine* which he later served as editor.

He entered World War I as a private with a hospital unit, transferred to the field artillery, saw active duty on the front, and emerged as captain. Having married in 1916, he could have been exempted from service but entered from "a conscientious fulfillment of duty." His first volume of poetry, *Tower of Ivory*, appeared in 1917 while he was in France. After the war he earned a law degree with highest honors at Harvard and taught there for one year. He spent the following three years with the distinguished law firm of Charles F. Choate, Jr., in Boston. His real interest, however, was in poetry.

During the winter of 1923, he left for France with his wife and two children. He has said of this decision that it marked "the beginning of my more or less adult life." He spent the next five years in Paris, St. Cloud, on the Mediterranean, in Normandy, one spring in Persia, and occasional summers in the Berkshires in Massachusetts. France has always been hospitable to artists, to experiments in art forms, to the interplay of the arts, to the development of movements. MacLeish found congenial environment and began to read the nineteenth-century French poets who had been exciting creative minds, as well as Ezra Pound and T. S. Eliot, "exponents of the current philosophy of despair."

For the next thirty years MacLeish was to find that whatever he wrote was to be subjected to critics who felt they could recognize an influence, hear an echo of a familiar metrical pattern, suspect a mood, recall a theme or symbol or some technical device. If he did try his wings according to what he learned from one writer or another, he very early worked out his own poetic forms. He wrote during these early years in Paris a number of fine lyrics which won him a place in American poetry. Even then his independent spirit protected him from being merely an imitator, or from being "taken in" by the literary fads for which Paris is famous. A comment made three decades later about this Paris education illustrates the point: "When I set myself, after college and after law school, to try to find my way to a place where I could begin, I taught myself Italian enough to read *The Divine Comedy* because Tom Eliot had read it to his great profit and because I was—as I remain—his devoted admirer. It did me, I am sure, no harm. But neither did it do me Eliot's good, for it was not my need that took me to it."[3] His long poem, *The Hamlet of A. MacLeish* (1928), marks the end of the deep self-searching which characterized his Paris years.

In 1928 MacLeish and his family returned to America to a Massachusetts farm. The first volume on his return, *New Found Land* (1930), includes some poems written in Europe, some in America. In spite of being torn between the old world and the new, he obviously was seeking a sense of direction, an identification with his own country. The volume marks a continued interest in craftsmanship and an increased skill in a variety of forms. His position as editor of *Fortune,* beginning in 1930, was a significant departure from the perspective and kind of writing which had held his attention in the 1920's. His associations were with men in business and in high offices and with factual materials belonging to the world of finance and government.

From the firsthand knowledge gained on a trip to Mexico and from the reading of the Bernal Díaz account of the conquest under Cortés, he wrote the lyric-epic, *Conquistador* (1932), a poem directed to a wider audience than the early lyrics and, consequently, more widely read. It won for him his first Pulitzer Prize. This poem and *Frescoes for Mr. Rockefeller's City* (1933) involved him in controversy with the left-wing critics whom he answered both in verse and prose. These replies indicate his thinking about the nature of poetry and the relation of the poet to his time.

The first anthology, *Poems 1924-1933*, represents ten years of experimentation in verse forms and, according to many critics, a reflection of his wide reading and acquaintance in English and French poetry. This volume also indicates a break from this tutelage, a return to America and a deep concern with the American heritage. In addition, it represents the early awareness of the political climate and the disastrous turn of events in Europe, as in the poem "1933." During the later 1930's Mac-Leish continued to turn his attention to the world about him, directed his poetry to a wider audience, and wrote three short plays and poems that were frankly public speech. During these years he continued to write personal lyrics, just as he had in the 1920's.

After a year at Harvard as "Curator" of the Nieman Foundation, he entered public life as Librarian of Congress where he served from 1939 to 1944. During the latter of these years he was also director of the Office of Facts and Figures, and later assistant director in the Office of War Information. A fluent and persuasive speaker, he was in continual demand; and, as a man deeply concerned about the crises of the world at war, he made tireless use of his writing talent to alert the country to the issues at stake. In *The Irresponsibles* he attacked the "ivory-tower" detachment of many of his fellow writers who did not involve themselves with issues that threatened to destroy their world. Two collections of essays, *A Time to Speak* (1941) and *A Time to Act* (1942) are a partial record of these years when he was also involved in the vast work of reorganizing the Library of Congress. At the end of the war he participated in the establishing of the United Nations Educational Scientific and Cultural Organization; he set up the constitution and served as chairman of the program committee which had to coordinate plans for world-wide cultural activities. *Actfive* (1948), a volume of poems written during these years, reflects the concerns of a man heavily dedicated to public work and public speech. This volume is important in the record of a poet who believed that his own poetry should be of the world in which he lived.

Appointed Boylston Professor of Poetry and Rhetoric in 1949 at Harvard University, where he served until his retirement in 1962, he continued to state his position on major issues facing the mid-twentieth century. *The Trojan Horse* (1952), written at the height of the McCarthy controversy, and *Poetry and Opinion* (1950), written as an apology for poetry for our time after the row over the Bollingen Award to Ezra Pound, are two examples. The second and more complete anthology, *Collected Poems 1917-1952*, which won for him a second Pulitzer Prize, gave the reader a perspective on the range and stature of his poetry and enabled critics to re-evaluate their judgments of his work as a whole. He returned to the tradition of fine lyrics, so much admired in the earlier collections, with the slender but rich *Songs for Eve* (1954).

MacLeish reached Broadway in 1959 with *J. B.*, a modern version of the Book of Job, that won him a third Pulitzer Prize and aroused controversy both as to religious interpretation and art form. Out of his teaching and lectures came an original approach to the "means to meaning" in poems, *Poetry and Experience* (1961). The sum total of a half-century's work from the first lyric in the *Yale Literary Magazine* in October, 1911, to the book about poetry in 1961 is a considerable record.

Throughout the multiple careers and commitments to issues of his own time, he has developed a clearly stated position of what the poet's role in America should be. He belongs to the tradition of Yeats, of St.-John Perse, of Tu Fu, and of other poets who have engaged in public affairs and who have written poetry that spoke to their own time.

CHAPTER 2

Poet and 'Expatriate'

I

THE EARLY POETRY of Archibald MacLeish is representative of undergraduate verse at the time of World War I. The poems emerge from dreams and intuition rather than from experience, and they reflect the literary interests of his college years. He was a frequent contributor to the *Yale Literary Magazine* beginning with "Gifts" in the October, 1911, issue. Many of these poems appeared in the first volume, *The Tower of Ivory* (1917), collected by a Yale friend, Lawrence Mason, when MacLeish was serving with the United States Army in France. Written in a conscious literary tone, they convey the detachment of the poet's point of view. In his Introduction, Mason says: "Under various symbols he is passionately appealing for the intuitive apprehension of reality as against the baffling limitations of the reason and the senses."[1] "Baccalaureate" with its "shard of broken memories" conveys the poet's regret for the transient in college intellectual life and emotional experiences. "Our Lady of Troy," a dramatic scene in blank verse about the Faust legend, probably reflects a student's reading of Marlowe as well as a Dutch translation of an original source. The final poem, "Realities," also carries the Faustian themes of bartering and of disillusionment over the mind's limitations.

As a college student, MacLeish, like Yeats, began writing poetry in the Romantic tradition. The years in France and the post-war return to America destroyed the "ivory-tower" perspective. There were a number of factors to influence a young man who took poetry seriously: the impact of the war itself, the loss of a brother and friends, an attempt to adjust to a profession unsuited to his temperament, and living in a decade of shifting values and new freedom, a time friendly neither to poetry nor to poets.

In the early 1920's he was published in *Parabalou,* a pamphlet of poems by younger American poets.[2] Some of the poems reflect the war experience. "A Belgian Letter," in heroic couplets, describes a sixty-year-old Flemish merchant whose sons have all been killed and who comes upon the body of an American soldier. A poem, "Kenneth," about his brother killed in Belgium, praises his zest for life and describes his death as "washed clean in anger and the fighter's pride." In "Creation," a conversation between the poet and God about the time before creation, God must admit his ignorance. Some poems are frankly humorous, as is "Invocation" which mocks at beauty; others attempt to recall memories. Many are in conventional quatrains, some are experiments in two and three-beat lines, a number are sonnets. When MacLeish was writing these poems, he was finishing his law degree, was teaching, and was practicing law. His real interest, however, was poetry.

After World War I, Europe became a gathering place for artists and writers seeking a congenial place in which to work. France, always hospitable to the creative spirit, became the home of those in search of new forms, new ways of expressing what they had to say. When the post-war rash of young writers, college graduates between the years 1915-22, left philistine America for more congenial Paris, Pound made his escape. Gertrude Stein, who had come to Paris before Pound, called this second wave of "expatriates" by a name that was to emerge as an emblem, "a lost generation." She became a kind of rallying figure for the artists and writers of the 1920's. Most of these later Americans were financially able to devote full time to writing and friendships. Wrenched from their own tradition, disillusioned and unprepared for the world after the war, they wrote nostalgic books about their childhood, or bitter accounts of their war years.

Archibald MacLeish became one of these so-called "expatriates." For five years he was part of this literary coterie; read the French poets; became deeply engrossed in the work of Ezra Pound and T. S. Eliot; became acquainted with other young writers who also had come out of the war disillusioned, uprooted, torn from traditional roots, and wrote poetry.

In these years he learned metrics from the school of Pound and Eliot, from Laforgue and other French poets. He achieved mastery in getting at the root meaning of words, and developed a cadence and rhythm of his own. He was able to weather a barrage of artistic manifestoes delivered in Paris because, from these earlier years, he was suspicious of clichés and of any attempt to accommodate writing to a special ideology. He tried a number of styles, he adapted to his own use a number of verse forms, he reinterpreted myth in terms of his own experience, and he repeatedly gave to personal experience a larger significance. There appear to be echoes from the poets and poems he studied, and reflections in his own poems of the thinking and mood of the decade in which he was writing. From the beginning, critics have tried to pinpoint indebtedness. But while they were judging, MacLeish moved on to hammer out his own individual style, to test themes and forms, and to achieve a body of work that is distinctive.

The volumes of the 1920's represent several stages in Mac-Leish's "intellectual Anabasis." The college volume, *Tower of Ivory* (1917), echoes the Romantic stock-in-trade of the time. *The Happy Marriage* (1924), seeming to reflect reading in Donne and other metaphysical poets but also suggesting an intensely personal reference, marks a significant development in form and intensity. *Streets in the Moon* (1926), reflecting the variety of influence under which he worked, has been called "almost a laboratory notebook of experiments." *Nobodaddy*, published in 1926 but written before 1925, shows great increase in poetic power and technique. *The Pot of Earth* (1925) and *The Hamlet of A. MacLeish* (1928) show the influence of Eliot, and the latter perhaps even more the influence of St.-John Perse. It was *The Hamlet* that first attracted critics, for it seemingly mirrored the prevailing mood of the "lost generation."

II The Happy Marriage (1924)

The title poem, "The Happy Marriage," suggests that the young poet shifted his interest from the British nineteenth century to the poets of the seventeenth, Donne and other members of the metaphysical school. This sequence, much tighter and more subtle than the college verse, written in sonnet and various other forms, represents a considerable technical advance. In a series of paradoxes the poems describe the subtle relationships between a man and wife, the separateness in intimacy, the play of desire and surfeit, the intuitive understanding and the doubt, satisfaction and discontent, the dream and the awareness of time, beauty, and death.

The first unit, built on the familiar Renaissance contrast of microcosm and macrocosm, describes man and woman as separate as two nations, as distant as two stars, in spite of their physical union. The second unit conveys the paradox that man is immortal, woman mortal; that woman's flesh, like a tree, rises in each new generation, that man is the "Vain leaves that gild her summer"; that man marries his dreams, and woman "her man for evil or for good." The third, a sonnet, expresses the idea that marriage which spends itself in passion is only "love's true negative"; but "the ever unpossessed" is not love either. The seventh poem of the sequence offers an interesting and early experiment in rhythms and verbal duplication:

> Beside her in the dark the chime
> Of ratcheted resolving time
> Repeating its repeated beat
> Builds complicated incomplete
> Sonatas in his listening brain . . .

The final unit illustrates, in another paradox, what was to become characteristic of MacLeish, the restatement of an old myth in a new metaphor:

> Beauty is that Medusa's head
> Which men go armed to seek and sever:
> It is most deadly when most dead,
> And dead will stare and sting forever—
> Beauty is that Medusa's head.

The sense of the transitory quality of love, of beauty, and of life, the search for the perfect relationship without the old faith in intuition reflect the temper not only of MacLeish at this time but of his contemporaries in the twenties.

III Nobodaddy (1925-26)

Two longer works, *The Pot of Earth* (1925) and *Nobodaddy* (1926—written before 1925), reflect a new point of view and an acquaintance with a different kind of poetry: a reading in Pound and Eliot, in the metaphysical poetry of the seventeenth century, and perhaps in the work of the French anti-Romantic poets. The little verse play, hardly a drama, deserves particular attention because of the similarity between the serpent voice in *Nobodaddy* and that of Mr. Nickles of *J. B.*, and the resemblance

between the attitudes of Cain and those of J. B., the moderniza-
tion of the Job character.

As epigraph to *Nobodaddy* MacLeish quotes from William
Blake:

> Why art thou silent and invisible,
> Father of Jealousy?
> Why dost thou hide thyself in the clouds—

Blake's views are of particular interest here. He said that in
orthodox religion, in "official Christianity" that is, God is good
and yet allots to man, who is evil, calamities and miseries; God's
special servants set up rituals for man to follow obediently. In
this state, religion and visions of poets and prophets are of no
account. This concept of God as a god of mystery and power
and cruelty represents the worst of man's ideas of deity. Those
who worship this God are really worshiping the devil. Blake
calls this orthodox concept, "Old Nobodaddy"; it is an idea of
a personal god but also of an impersonal force when it relapses
into Fate or Necessity. Because man is a fallen creature, according to this theology, he must look beyond the human world for
salvation; "and there is nothing beyond the human world except
the spatial beyond which is nature, and which suggests all
these ideas of uncritical docility. Hence routine and passive
life come to be thought good; all that is independent, free and
energetic comes to be associated with evil."[3]

Blake also believed that this same conventional element in
society created the idea of predestination and set up a morality
based on a worship of mediocrity. This orthodox idea of God
and man makes of Satan not a sinner but an unbeliever; he is
the questioner who is always drawing man into a state of
mind commonly thought of as sin. In a kind of world where
man cannot approach the oracles, his power of becoming good
must be within himself. And this final point brings the poet
Blake and the author of *Nobodaddy* and *J. B.* close together.

MacLeish describes in the earlier verse play the predicament
of an independent mind in a world of orthodox religious belief.
In the Introduction, he says he does not treat the Garden of
Eden legend as metaphor but has given arbitrary significance
to incidents in the story in order to dramatize "the condition of
self-consciousness in an indifferent universe." The form of the
play has been likened to Yeats's *Four Plays for Dancers*, written
after his study of the Japanese Noh plays. R. P. Blackmur

wrote of *Nobodaddy* in terms of conventional drama: he found neither argument nor discussion in the play, only "attitudes presented with the force of poetry, not ideas demonstrated by logic."[4]

MacLeish presents the different states of mind of Adam and Eve in and outside the Garden of Eden, achieving a dramatic climax in the third act with the clash between two points of view represented by the orthodox Abel and the independent Cain. Nobodaddy is the gardener in Eden who brings the fertilizing rain. He seems to be subject to the sun he himself created, unable to prevent the death of his creation, Behemoth, the beast mentioned in the Book of Job. He gave to the ants and bees a semblance of mind but withheld understanding. Adam and Eve know him as the wind, a movement of the leaves or as a felt presence. Satan is represented by the Voice, at first as an echo in Adam's own head, later in Adam's words, and later still by the words which Cain asserted in greater independence of Old Nobodaddy. Satan's role as tempter is to raise in Adam's mind doubts of God's power, awareness of the possibilities of his own mind, and the conviction that he, too, can be a god and build his own world. Cain, almost as if extending the serpent's inquiry, raises questions about the kind of god which will destroy the good and innocent, the kind of god that demands blood sacrifice from his worshipers.

In the Garden of Eden, cool and green, Adam and Eve have lived in timelessness and innocence, wary only of the tree. The serpent voice questions God's way when he says to Adam, "You have that in you which could build a world," a talent that is hidden in his dark body. The serpent urges him to defy God and death. Taking courage from the serpent's words, Adam says the old god is jealous of man's mind: "He knew that if we ate we should be gods / Stronger than he is." In spite of his brave words, Adam is dominated by the old fears. In the mythical pantomime—eating the apple—Eve is surprised that she is not struck dead; she experiences only knowledge of herself and of Adam; she experiences a feeling of shame.

The Eliot influence is apparent in the second act which opens in a kind of wasteland, a dusty area adjacent to Eden. In lines that are reminiscent of Wordsworth's "Ode on Intimations of Immortality" but written in the tone of the disillusioned 1920's, Adam struggles to recall "Faces he once knew" with "their blinded eyes, their eyes of earth, of stone" which now frighten him. Isolated from Eden, Adam and Eve recall the green grass, the rain, and the animals. The present is "a staring backward into sleep," an awareness that all is strange, dangerous, secret; they are in a place of "darkness listening." In this world of desolation and silence, Adam, bereft of the supporting voice of Satan and obsessed with guilt, presents himself to God as a sinner, and waits for his punishment. There is no sound. The guilt-driven first parents go beyond the wall where no living things grow because, as Eve says, "There are no ways for us."

The conflict between the orthodox and the independent mind, suggested in the first act, culminates in the third. Cain at thirty-five describes Abel as more leopard than man, his mind "a tree's mind," his thought "like the sap." Cain is different: "I think about myself. I think of my thoughts. / I think of things that I can see." Because he thinks as a man, there is no communication between the brothers. Cain envisions a very different kind of a world, not "this earth, this desert." The frightened Eve warns Cain that God will destroy him for his pride, that Cain cannot bring rain or save a sheep choking for water. Cain replies that the desert belongs to God: "The drouth is his / But I can pity the poor beasts that die; / He cannot." Cain further answers Eve, fearful of his independence:

> Godhead is in me blossoming. Not dread,
> Not awe, nor power over suns and stars,
> But godhead, godhead to be pitiful,
> Godhead to laugh—

Recalling Adam's similar once-proud dream, she describes his present fearfulness: "He clings to me among the leaves until / Sleep hides him from himself." Cain repeats his certainty that man must serve God within himself and not the God in trees.

The play achieves its real dramatic climax when Abel, a ram slung over his shoulder, returns from the edge of Eden where he called to God but got no answer. He is about to sacrifice the sheep. Cain objects to this senseless killing; he protests that the ram has done no harm, is not responsible for the drought. Abel is certain that God will be pleased with the sacrifice; Cain offers the dried beans and withered corn that Abel's God has destroyed. Abel expresses belief in the god of wrath who made all things and demands man's supplication—Blake's Nobodaddy. Cain rejects a god of vengeance that demands submissive obedience:

> If we bow
> We'll never stand upright on earth again.
> The things that serve him go on knuckle bones
> Turning their backs upon the light. Crawl, crawl,
> Crawl if you love him. Or on your hands and knees
> Crawl back to Eden. Bow like a beast, he'll give you
> Water enough...

As Abel is about to make the sacrifice, Cain observes the ram's trusting look: "Only God can kill the things / That trust him." Cain rebels at the primitive ceremony, at the forces that would drag him down groveling, against "an unknown something... [that] darkens the scared brain." When Abel's supplications seem to be answered by thunder and rain, Cain refuses to be moved. When Abel tries to force Cain down to his own level of fear, Cain strikes him with the sacrificial knife. Stunned that God does not destroy him for killing his priest, and asking whether he is grown too small for God's concern, Cain cries out, "I stand against you cursing you. Lift up, / Lift up your hand and slay me." There is only silence. Cain, as did Adam before him, runs blindly and lost, calling for some kind of response: "Where are you, god? Where are you, god? / Speak to me—"

R. P. Blackmur contrasted Abel, the fanciful mystic, with Cain the zealous apostle of reason. He praised the third scene. He thought that from the entry of Abel, the play was drama at its best. Through the antithesis of Abel and Cain, God was both worshiped and defied: "Man is the ruin as well as the triumph of God." He felt that the poet had not fulfilled the character of Eve, had not exhausted the possibility of her relationship to her two sons.[4] MacLeish was to develop the central problem of the play when he adapted the story of Job, and he was to restate the central theme again in *Songs for Eve*.

IV The Pot of Earth

The Pot of Earth, said to have been written after the death of a son, has been likened to *The Waste Land*, though it would seem to be closer in spirit to the lines in *Sweeney Agonistes*: "Birth, copulation, and death / That's all, that's all, that's all, that's all." Both Eliot and MacLeish made use of ancient myth from Frazer and wrote with the disillusionment of the 1920's. It has been said that Eliot's poem is "a critique of our own day" but that MacLeish "finds one major symbol of the tragic predicament of all mortals" and relates the Adonis legend to the story of a modern girl.[5] Whereas Eliot devised a complicated interrelation of symbols, significances, and references from many sources, MacLeish focused upon one major symbol of birth, death, and resurrection. Like Eliot, he places in juxtaposition the ancient and contemporary, a technique reminiscent of Jules Laforgue.[6] MacLeish seems not to be too much interested in secret symbols; he relates the modern tale against the background of ancient myth and gives to it the significance of an ever-repeated and always universal experience.

Two epigraphs set the scheme of the poem.[7] The first is Frazer's description of the gardens of Adonis—pots sown with grains and flowers, "fostered by the sun's heat"; after being tended for eight days by women, the rootless and sallow plants are then thrown into the sea along with images of Adonis. The second epigraph is Hamlet's advice to Polonius not to let his daughter "walk i' the sun," a bitter comment that sets the tone of the poem.

MacLeish relates his three-part statement about the girl's youth, motherhood, and death to the ancient myth of the life cycle in both vegetable and animal worlds. He dramatizes the human condition in terms of building, maturity, and decay in the world of plants. He gives a particularly modern twist to the primitive myth by making his poem the psychological probing of a girl into her own destiny. Scenes symbolic of nature's annual sequence as well as certain stages in the girl's life are presented through her consciousness and her own reactions.

Part I, "Sowing of the Dead Corn," opens with the image of the dead Adonis drifting on a rudderless barge down the fallen tide of the Nile. The first scene pictures the girl watching her father, as if he were repeating the ancient rite, throwing "the dead stalks of last year's corn / Over the wall into the sea." The return of spring in the vegetable and animal kingdom is related to the girl's fearful emergence into puberty. The poet's reinterpretation of the old myth of death and resurrection[8] is combined with an image, recurring in the poem, of the fertilizing property of water:

> And after the rain the brook in the north ravine
> Ran blood-red—after the rain they found
> Purple hepaticas and violets.

The burgeoning forces of nature, bent on their endless cycle, are paralleled by the seventeen-year-old girl's urge to wait, to try to find a meaning to the cycle of birth, flowering, and death. The choice between life and sterility is expressed in the contrast between the buds on the chestnut tree and the salt stone cast up by the sea which does not "fructify." The girl's awakening to love is conveyed by a few images: a jostling in a railroad station, scraps of colloquial speech, a pounding in her throat, a questioning whether "he" has come and gone. This fragmentary handling of the scene, with its emphasis on connotative and impressionistic detail, its focus on consciousness, and its attention to contemporary speech recalls the technique of Jules Laforgue. It was also characteristic of this Impressionistic French poet to relate ancient myth to modern times.[9]

The modern rites of spring are suggested by an Easter Sunday's outing at Hooker's Grove—a blend of references to the Adonis myth, fragments of colloquial idiom, and impressions filtered through the girl's consciousness. Her awareness of changes in herself ranges from emotions of near weeping to wonder, from listening to "a girl calling her lost cows," to watching "oak-trees / Oozing new green at the tips of them. . . ." The relation between the world of nature and her own development is symbolized in the parallel rites of spring: "On the third day / The cone of the pine is broken" and with the girl, "Well, it was like a dream, / It happened so quickly, all of a sudden it happened—"

Part II, "The Shallow Grass," opens with an image of the girl as a sacrificial symbol. The parallels between nature and the girl are specific: in the ancient fertility rites the earth is prepared for the seeds; black oxen "shod with brass" drag a plough "shared with black copper." The young couple depart for their wedding night: "He can't keep his / Hands off her. Ripe as a peach she is."[10] From the train window she watches the plowed fields, "Rigid, with long welts, with open wounds." As he talks of the bridal chamber and a private supper, her mind races from girlish illusions to disillusionment and ugliness—"the chalked letters"—to a feeling "like the warmth of the sun driving / Downward into her heart."

Images of the gardens of Adonis are equated with the girl's pregnancy. The sprouting grass in her window box grew "a sort of whitey yellowy all / Fluffy" and she thought of hairs growing out of her own dead skull—an image worthy of T. S.

Eliot. Meditating upon her condition, she describes herself as "a handful / Of fat mold breeding corruption."[11] The ruthless drive of nature, bent only on reproduction, rouses in the girl a sense of rebellion. As she waits for the birth of her child, she hears "the wind whispering," something she could not and would not understand. Her condition is paralleled to that in the vegetable world: "The summer sucking through a withered straw / Enough stale water for a few beans." She sees herself as "a room at the end of a long journey," a room opening upon night or nothing; she describes herself as a woman walking in the autumn rain by "charnel fields" of rotting corn, "and livid, broken skulls / Of cabbages." To be a woman is to be "A naked body born to bear / Nakedness suffering."

Part III, "The Carrion Spring," opens with a symbolic reference to the Adonis legend: "The flowers of the sea are blown / Dead, they blossom in death." After the birth of her son, the girl listens to the cry of the sea calling her home: "Empty, gleaned, a reaped meadow / Fearing the rain no more" nor the flood tides "with their generative waters." She asks for a secret burial where the rain cannot "breed from me some living thing again."

The poet observes that spring did blossom again, "a cold / Bubbling of the corrupted pool." The poet offers to conduct the reader into the closed tomb and to show him the mystery of the dead god resurrected, "the reaped ear / Sprouting." The girl's rebellion over nature's ruthless demand to fructify—the role of woman as womb—gives another meaning to the Adonis legend. It was to become characteristic of MacLeish to reinterpret myths, legends, and beliefs that have become accepted in traditional ways.

The Pot of Earth represents a considerable technical advance. It may be that MacLeish did learn from Laforgue and Pound the value of myth; from Laforgue he developed an interest in language as well as psychology, and from Eliot the rich connotative power of symbolism. He had at this time achieved a sensitivity to the use of language, and had developed a facility for creating a musical line. He had forged variations in verse patterns to suit different moods: blank verse, two-beat or irregular five-beat lines, lines fragmented; free verse segments, three quatrains, long lines alternated with one-beat lines; rhymes occasionally, at other times lines paired with assonance and alliteration, as for instance, "hand full:" "seed fall"; or repetitions with slight variations, "fetid smell," the "live smell"; or internal rhymes and alliteration, "odor of blossoms. She half drowsed. She dreamed." He used "s"-sounds to convey the sensory impression of bursting summer: "Construe the soundless, slow / Explosion of a summer cloud, decipher / The sayings of the wind. ..."

The first stanza recalls the syntax of Yeats and other modern poets who, by delaying the subject, maintain a suspense until the image is completely projected. There is also repetition of an image, sometimes with a slight variation, for musical effect or for emphasis: "the singing on the mountain"; "the voices singing"; "with songs"—in three consecutive lines; or "earth loosened," "the earth relaxed." Another indication of development is the evidence of condensation; for instance, in an older edition of *The Pot of Earth* an additional character, a Syrian immigrant, gives the bloodroot flower to the girl.

V   Streets in the Moon (1926)

This early volume, *Streets in the Moon,* did not receive the attention it deserved until the publication of the first anthology, *Poems 1924-1933;* but it includes some of the most highly regarded lyrics that MacLeish has written. It has been commended for its variety of subjects and for the different patterns of verse, the precision and ease of the different rhythms, the evocative quality of the imagery, and lines memorable as song. Many of these poems reflect disillusionment and bitterness from the war experience, a deep concern over man's inability to know the universe and find a meaning for his own place in it, and a rejection of the values of an industrial society.

A number of the poems are elegies. "The Silent Slain" makes an analogy between the soldiers killed in World War I and the men of Roland trapped at Roncevaux. The effect of sustained lament is gained by a single continuing statement in regular iambic pentameter broken and left suspended at the end of the poem. The slow and deliberate opening lines have the sound of mourning: "We too, we too, descending once again / The hills of our own land. ..." The final words accentuate the procession-like dirge of the lines themselves, and the sounds of the words are in keeping with the revelation of treachery:

> And crossed the dark defile at last, and found
> At Roncevaux upon the darkening plain
> The dead against the dead and on the silent ground
> The silent slain—

"1892-19—" in a matter-of-fact juxtaposition of images comments on the brevity of life and the certainty of oblivion. There is no comforting retreat into immortality. "Three words the world knows— / Little enough to forget." The poem with startling candor describes death in patterned lines:

> It will be easy enough to forget.
> The rain drips
> Through the shallow clay,
> Washes lips,
> Eyes, brain,
> The rain drips in the shallow clay,
> The soft rain will wash them away—

"Interrogate the Stones" is composed of a series of questions about whether death is the answer. A curious image in the second stanza gains tension by the sense of its impending presence. Again the stanza form, a delicate balance of paired lines, of rhymes, of participles, and of alliteration within the line, reveals a close attention to form:

> But—have you heard
> That other endless asking? Have you seen
> The stale ironic question lean
> At evening from a window-place
> To face
> The coming in of night, or stand
> Where the sea breaks upon the broken land
> Hour by hour listening?

"Immortal Helix" describes the apparently insignificant life of one Jacob Schmidt, or perhaps many men. This amusing epitaph, characteristic of the wry humor the reader comes to expect of MacLeish, reports that he "Has been his hundred times around the sun," keeps endlessly spinning, and even his "Dead bones roll on." "Mistral over the Graves" is another experiment in repetitions, but it is interesting for the labials and sibilants chosen to describe this cold dry wind that blows over the Mediterranean: "Be still—listen to the wind! / Listen to the night wind slithering and splashing / In the palm trees...." "Signature for Tempo," which recalls the sonnet of Donne about "the numberless infinities / Of souls" undone by death, makes use of the image of an endlessly whirling universe and of man being caught in a world perpetually falling but motionless, of man having some sense of the past but very little of the future.

One of the most frequently quoted poems in the volume is the very moving elegy, "Memorial Rain," written for his brother Kenneth MacLeish, killed in Belgium, 1918. Against the fulsome words of the Ambassador, the wind, like a monster—"a heavy drag / Of wind," or "The wind coiled... dragging its heavy body"—is finally dispelled by the rain. The sense of kinship between the poet and his brother buried in a strange land increases with the monstrous wind and the banal, dishonest words of the memorial speech. The mounting tension of the poet, aware of the brother, stranger in a foreign grave, waiting, listening, is dispelled by the rain which tramples the wind and scatters the insensitive who listen to the bombast. The rain leaves the dead at peace with the earth. The long declarative sentences at first carry their slow rhythms like a funeral dirge. Line after line evokes the sound of the wind and the sense of waiting, listening; a feeling of suspense is achieved partly by the sound of the words, partly by the verbal forms.

> I had not slept for knowing
> He too, dead, was a stranger in that land
> And felt beneath the earth in the wind's flowing
> A tightening of roots and would not understand,
> Remembering lake winds in Illinois,
> That strange wind.

In strange and bitterly ironic words—*"in French, felicitous tongue"*—the Ambassador mouths the country's gratitude to *"these happy, happy dead."* The sudden relief which brings to an end both wind and rhetoric is expressed in rapid staccato lines:

> The living scatter, they run into houses, the wind
> Is trampled under the rain, shakes free, is again
> Trampled.

A number of poems in this volume express the feeling common to the post-war writers: rootlessness in the immediate world and a sense of frustration deriving from vast areas of knowledge—scientific knowledge for the most part—which had disrupted the accepted concept of the universe. "L'an Trentiesme de Mon Eage"—the title a line from Pound's "Hugh Selwyn Mauberley"—describes one who has come by lost ways and asks how he is to return as "the unknown constellations sway." Morton Zabel in 1930 called this poem "the pivot of ... [MacLeish's] subsequent thought." He believed that his work was an attempt to answer his own question of how to go back.[12] I. L. Solomon called it a fine poem but thought it came by way of Pound's "Mauberley" and that it reflected the influence of Eliot in "wordplay" and tone.[13]

The sense of alienation, of being unprotected by orthodox religion, a sense of lostness which preoccupies modern man is stated in the sonnet, "End of the World." It may be said to represent a theme not only of the 1920's but also of some of MacLeish's own writing in later decades. If there are no answers to the mysteries, if there is no defense in the elaborate rituals and disciplines of the church, man must rely on the gift of the divine within his own mind. Amos Wilder referred to "the tone of mock fantasy" with which the idea of a silent, indifferent universe is projected in the image of a circus tent,[14] an image that was later to provide the setting for *J. B.*:

> Quite unexpectedly at Vasserot
> The armless ambidextrian was lighting
> A match between his great and second toe
> And Ralph the lion was engaged in biting
> The neck of Madame Sossman while the drum
> Pointed, and Teeny was about to cough
> In waltz-time swinging Jocko by the thumb—
> Quite unexpectedly the top blew off:
>
> And there, there overhead, there, there, hung over
> Those thousands of white faces, those dazed eyes,
> There in the starless dark the poise, the hover,
> There with vast wings across the canceled skies,
> There in the sudden blackness the black pall
> Of nothing, nothing, nothing—nothing at all.

"Lines for a Prologue," "Mother Goose's Garland," "Nocturne," "Selene Afterwards"—all interesting for their technical experiments—are other comments on man's life as senseless maundering. "Le Secret Humain" and "Le seul malheur est que je ne sais pas lire" suggest the mystery, man's groping, and his occasional intimation of final knowledge.

A few poems in the volume are portraits. "The Farm" describes in a series of vignettes dated from 1750 to 1923 a pioneer New

England family that broke the wilderness and lived out its line. "Eleven," a more fully delineated portrait, excellent for its insight into the sensitive mind of a child, describes the intuitive communication between a boy and an old gardener. "Sketch for a Portrait of G—M—," reminiscent of E. A. Robinson, describes a person through associations, memories, and feelings connected with her room.

Four comments on contemporary society reveal the poet's vigorous sense of humor. "Verses for a Centennial," in rhythms and colloquial speech suggestive of Carl Sandburg, jests with those who would transfix an artist or a philosopher to a definite time and place. "Man!" ridicules in advertiser's clichés the predilection for easy panaceas. The poem is obviously a parody but some critics have treated it with heavy solemnity. "Corporate Entity," a sonnet that derives its special, comic effect by a single, unpunctuated statement of detailed names and objects, satirizes the profitable business of cheap, art reproductions. "Hearts and Flowers" is a witty excursion into free verse that achieves a delicately smooth movement from the labial sounds. The poem describes the fertilization of the sea anemone but cloaks the sexual act in exotic, technical vocabulary. By means of unusual word play the poet seems to be having his private joke with the scientists.

"Ars Poetica" has been called MacLeish's ultimate expression of the art-for-art's-sake tenet. Taken as one statement of his theory, the poem does defy the "hair splitting analysis of modern criticism." Written in three units of double-line stanzas and in rhyme, it makes the point that a poem is an intimation rather than a full statement, that it should "be motionless in time"; that it has no relation to generalities of truth, historical fact, or love—variations, perhaps, of truth, beauty, and goodness. The third stanza reads:

> A poem should be equal to:
> Not true.
>
> For all the history of grief
> An empty doorway and a maple leaf.
>
> For love
> The leaning grasses and two lights above the sea—
>
> A poem should not mean
> But be.

VI Einstein

The poem *Einstein* (1929), originally included in *Streets in the Moon,* not only suggests a brilliant mind working to penetrate the mysteries of the universe and to define its law but also implies a warm human being, a small man "solidly contracted into space." As in the previous longer poems, *Nobodaddy* and *The Pot of Earth,* MacLeish devises a number of scenes in which the scientist struggles with unanswerable problems much like those of his own as a poet. He describes Einstein as "something inviolate," a concentration in the infinities of time and space:

> Extensively the universe itself,
> Or chronologically the two dates
> Original and ultimate of time . . .

As if defining the limits of man's knowledge, he notes that within the scientist's own boundaries, not a Jehovah, nor a million stars, nor all night's constellations can be contained; and yet he, as scientist, remains detached from "the revolutions of the stars."

The paradox of a human mind in a mindless universe is implied in his vision of the world as "rippling ether and the swarming motes" which makes shadows on his brain "In perpendiculars and curves and planes / And bodiless significances blurred. . . ." It may be the thing itself or subjective reality, "A world in reason which is in himself." Wherever he moves, "the world / Takes center and there circle round his head / Like golden flies in summer the gold stars." When his momentary grasp of truth disintegrates, he feels "The planet plunge beneath him," realizes that he knows "Less than a world and must communicate / Beyond his knowledge." At another moment his attempt at "essaying synthesis" is frustrated by his own physical awareness of the universe, by personal memories, by failure to find a word by which to translate a concept he almost grasps. In another pictured mental state there is partial communication in music, "Strange nameless words," that give an image to the ear but not to the brain. The poet recalls that the Virgin of Chartres knew a word, and that at one time there were words in Rome and Eleusis.

In still another scene the poet seems to be describing Einstein's wrestling with the concept that is popularly known as the unified field theory:

> He lies upon his bed
> Exerting on Arcturus and the moon
> Forces proportional inversely to
> The squares of their remoteness and conceives
> The universe.
> Atomic.
> He can count
> Oceans in atoms and weigh out the air
> In multiples of one and subdivide
> Light to its numbers.

The scientist remains determined to decipher their mysteries: "Solve them to unity."

In the final scene Einstein is pictured as standing on a windy slope, "And with his mind relaxes the stiff forms / Of all he sees. . . ." It is an image of change and dissolution:

> Still he stands
> Watching the vortex widen and involve
> In swirling dissolution the whole earth
> And circle through the skies till swaying time
> Collapses, crumpling into dark the stars . . .

Though he can see, "still the dark denies him," and though his own body also disintegrates, something living remains: "Something inviolate. A living something."

The poem communicates a sense of loneliness and frustration, of man's inability to understand his relationship to the universe. In spite of its failures, the reality of the human mind remains. MacLeish suggests in the poem what he feels a poem should be—the reality of feeling which may elude verbal expression. Stylistically, there are many interesting sections: for example, the attempt to translate the laws of physics into poetic images; the sense of movement and disintegration expressed in the final stanzas in verbs and participles: "overflow," "sweep," "crumble," "drown," "bubbling," "gathering," "ferment," "simmer."

Frederick J. Hoffman describes *Einstein* as "symbol of the self-defeating speculations of modern science." He describes the paradoxical position of the scientist who must reduce all his knowledge of the universe to abstractions which he can understand. In order to comprehend the great multiplicity of parts, he eliminates from each its individuality.[15] George Dangerfield wrote that *Einstein* was the first, full statement of a theme which excited MacLeish in these early years: "It is the lack of communication between man and the earth, the soil; it is the sense of earth's withdrawal, of earth's denial of itself to man; it is a perpetually unsatisfied desire to understand, to put into words, to rediscover the earth, the air, and the light."[16]

VII The Hamlet of A. MacLeish (1928)

Jules Laforgue, whose influence on the early work of both Pound and Eliot is said to be considerable, set a quotation from *Hamlet* as an epigraph to some of the poems in *Derniers Vers*. Laforgue, in widely different and original verse patterns, assumed the role of the Shakespearean character and wrote his own personal, introspective comments on the attitude and mores of his times.[17] In much the same way the poet in *The Hamlet of A. MacLeish* (1928) took from *Hamlet* a series of quotations which he used as frames, comparable to the epigraphs introducing *Nobodaddy* and *The Pot of Earth*. Within these Shakespearean frames, he places descriptions of psychological types and sets certain philosophical problems.

The Hamlet of A. MacLeish was the poet's first major work to attract the attention of the critics. Amos Wilder likens the poem to *The Waste Land* in that both present "the eerie Odysseys and Anabases of the soul," all the maladies and influences which haunted the war generation: "the theme of the sterility of existence, the drought, the parchedness of our condition. Man in alienation from the world, the organic unities broken, inevitably finds the relish of experience gone and worse still his spirit dying of thirst." The whole theme of the MacLeish poem is "the curse that lights upon us from our fathers, from the past: Hamlet coerced by his father's ghost to carry on old feuds; youth not free but the slave of an ancient ill."[18]

As in T. S. Eliot, here also are to be found the theme of sterile existence, man's alienation because of broken traditions, and the images of barren areas, dry bones, and the cry of jackals. Repeated echoes in the characterization of the poet recall Eliot's ineffectual Prufrock. There is, however, a conspicuous difference between Eliot's impersonal statement on the social condition and MacLeish's forthright account of his own frustrating inquiries. Whereas *The Waste Land* is an impersonal statement, *The Hamlet of A. MacLeish* is a frank confession of personal experience and involvement. It is Mac-

Leish who is unafraid to fling a hopeless challenge to himself and to admit his frustration and despair.[19]

The poem opens on a note reminiscent of the sonnet, "The End of the World," the early play, *Nobodaddy*, and of *Einstein*, in which man questions "that vast silence overhead" and gets no answer at all. Secrets known to ancient goatherds that have come down only as confused words, "vanishing signals," are dramatized by a scene (number three) in which Bleheris describes his search and discovery. MacLeish, as Eliot is said to have done in *The Waste Land*, seems to have taken from Jessie L. Weston's *From Ritual and Romance* the idea that Bleheris the Welshman may have been the author of the original concept of the Grail legend: "At its root lies the record, more or less distorted, of an ancient Ritual, having for its ultimate object the initiation into the secret of the sources of Life, physical and spiritual."[20]

As MacLeish describes the scene, Bleheris (Gawain), as if reading from a very old page, speaks of his journey in search of the chalice. He describes in dramatic step-by-step movement his progress from the civilized areas at the shore to the primitive island, following a single light to an empty church where he saw a cup "Crimson and burning and a flame of candles / Burning before it." Bleheris, alone in this dank church at night, the water dripping, the candle flame limp, stares at the cup:

> Forefeeling terror heard the beast go back,
> Rear and a hoof ring striking, and looked up
> And saw come inward at that window place,
> Come from the plunging darkness into light,
> Loose fingers groping, cropped, no arm there, grey,
> The nails gone, shriveled, a dead hand, and droop
> And close about the vessel. And the flame
> Leapt and the night had all. Then silence. Then,
> Loud till the stone shook, lamentable, long
> As all the dead together, a great cry
> Shrieking with laughter:

Bleheris tells of running away choked by "the stench / Of death, of flesh rot," of finding in a clearing the storm gone and the stars out.

The poet raises questions of the meaning of Bleheris' reading, whether man is deceived, whether "this is other than we think,"

[45]

whether "The thing is evil" and whether the "Familiar gestures" and "half signs" or warm earth and stars are only false and deceive us. MacLeish's dramatic handling of the death image and rot suggests that he raises questions whether the death-resurrection legend may not be a false promise—or a false interpretation of the old goatherd's words.

Other scenes (numbers four, five, and six) set in the frame of Hamlet's colloquy with his father's ghost turn to the poet's own experience, his own premonitions of something unbearable happening, his awareness that there are "Ways of knowing what it is I am knowing" but of being unable to read what the words say. Lines which reflect MacLeish's own travels—imagery of streets, names, sensations—recorded with overtones of "The Song of J. Alfred Prufrock" suggest that his own experiences have kept their secret. The terrible struggle to get behind the words, to rediscover what may once have been known, preoccupies the poet. He questions the interpretations to be made of the enigmatic signs from nature. The poet has heard "The voices calling the small new name of god" answered with the cry of jackals. The poet speaks of his time as one in which the water is salt, where neither birds nor green flowers flourish. It is the desert reminiscent of *The Waste Land*.

The poet-Hamlet seems to modify the "To be or not to be" soliloquy (scene eight) by raising questions that sound very close to his own personal career.[21] He wonders whether he should expose his personal grief "for solemn fettered fools" to criticize and judge as rhetoric. He deplores the writer's habit of exploiting his own experience for profit:

> Oh shame, for shame to suffer it, to make
> A skill of harm, a business of despair,
> And like a barking ape betray us all
> For itch of notice.

He urges himself to be silent, to fear in secret lest the dreams that obsess him reflect an evil within himself, which, exposed, will damn him.

Just as Laforgue contrasted the introvert with the extrovert,[22] so does MacLeish contrast the introspective poet-Hamlet with an objective, visceral, erotic uncle-father (scene two), a striking vignette described appropriately in strong Anglo-Saxon rhythms. This aggressive, brassy character is likened to the sun:

> He roars from the splashed sea driving the
> Nude girls through the surf, striking their
> Golden rumps with the hand flat, deriding
> Shyness with lewd words. He is loud
> In the blown blue sky as the laughter of
> Fed kings under arbors.

It is this inveterate optimist who presumes to reveal the dark and advises "with blabbed loose / Light over water." The nephew equivocates, obsessed by "the knowledge of ill among us and the obligation to revenge."

The king's guilt (scene nine) not only is personal but is described as the inherited guilt of Western man, pushing aggressively west, plundering, exploiting, and leaving only a record of his march. It is an account involving millions, a crime of the forefathers who left only a trail of suffering and death: girls delivered, screaming, in the dark tents; horses left to drown in the slime; children's bodies left floating in the ooze; fat lands exploited and abandoned. Guilt belongs to these men of action so smugly sure of their limited understanding and of their acquisitive ambitions. Mason Wade, commenting on the personal, painful self-searching in this poem which MacLeish was later to condemn, finds St.-John Perse the most important influence. This scene may have a certain affinity with *Anabase,* the French poem, published in 1925.[23]

The poet-Hamlet, dark and moody, who would take his revenge against this insensitive man of action, is portrayed as indecisive and ineffectual, as distressed by the "giggle of the wind" and by the "snigger of the faint stars." In the Ophelia scene (seven) is introduced the idea of love sullied by Puritanical associations of shame, guilt, and rejection. Polonius, like the uncle-king represented by the sun image, equates love with lust:

> Let them be crushed with stones who are found together.
> Let their sex be consumed with lime and their bodies
> Burned on the roots of trees slabbered by cattle.

At Ophelia's death the poet queries whether man has not received answers to the wrong questions: "We recognize ourselves by the wrong laugh." He observes that man seeks a comforting word to obscure the mystery of death so that he can sustain his comfort and optimism.

[47]

Obsessed with the burdens of inherited guilt, Hamlet urges himself to "play the strong boy" and to rebuke his mother's lechery (scene eleven):

> Face the brassy
> Broad indecent fact and with ironical
> Contemptuous understanding take the world's
> Scut in your hands and name it!

MacLeish's poem closes (scenes thirteen and fourteen are in the frame of Ophelia's burial) on a note of deep personal loss—the death of a son, of a brother, of friends, an expression that is not a mere literary exercise in the elegiac but an evocation of deep personal grief:

> I'll be ox-chine nude,
> Quartered to cold bare bone. Look, behold me
> Bearing my dead son's body to the grave.

And again, of the brother:

> Spreading on my young
> My three times buried brother's stony grave
> The bone-pale scented violets...

and crying out in agony. Hamlet's hypersensitivity, "the sense of spiritual insecurity," is culminated in the final scene. The poet, sickened by the easy optimists and the extroverts, faces the need for resignation:

> It is time we should accept...
> *Thou wouldst not think*
> *How ill all's here about my heart!*

George Dangerfield found a complete revolution from *The Pot of Earth* to *Hamlet* with *Einstein* half way between: "We find an insistent desire to return to the innocent world, to establish an innocent communication between man and the natural world" where there is neither shame nor superstition nor hostility. "This desire is linked up with a sense of great loneliness, great terror, and great frustration... embodied in a perpetual question, a question which the poet seems unable to answer."[24] Rica Brenner described the poem as representing the extreme of MacLeish's self-probing: "poetic pictures of un-

connected meditations of a soul sensitive to world's upheavals."
She found the poem not a drama of action nor of ideas; its
coherence is derived from the "layers-of-consciousness method."[25]

Lewis Galantière, writing about *Hamlet* in April, 1929,
described MacLeish as "extremely sensitive to his time and its
perturbations" and the poem as "highly ingenious in construction, nearly impeccable in versification, and deeply moving in
emotional intensity." He rebuked the peevish critics who rejected
what might be called the authenticity of MacLeish's esthetic
emotion and who berated him for writing too much or too little
like Eliot. What the critics really disliked, said Galantière, was
that MacLeish "is extremely sensitive to his time and its perturbations," that he is "stirred by the vast upheavals of our
world, and the spiritual disquietude of what a clever, excitable
Welshman has called Western Man. The investigations of Freud,
the new anthropology, the questionings of physical science" are
to Mr. MacLeish what Montaigne was to Shakespeare. Galantière
believed that Rimbaud, Pound, Eliot, and St.-John Perse were
MacLeish's Marlowe and his Lyly, his Shakespeare and his
Webster.[26]

A quarter of a century later opinion about the *Hamlet* was
still strong and divided, with the balance favorable. Hayden
Carruth—commenting on the structure of *Hamlet* and other of
the longer poems, as being "hung on a structure outside themselves"—thought that this frame detracted from the interest in
the poem.[27] Solomon called the poem a "brilliant psychological
study" in which MacLeish "probes himself as poet and man,
and at odds with the materialism of the world, he makes poetic
order out of the chaos within him."[28] Richard Eberhart thought
that *Hamlet* stands up well—"dense, honest, and final."[29] Kimon
Friar referred to it as "that magnificent exercise in Elizabethan
rant and rhetoric."[30]

CHAPTER 3

The Poet's Rediscovery of America

I

WHEN HE RETURNED to America in 1928, MacLeish began a very different kind of literary life. As a member of the editorial board of *Fortune* from its beginning, he was associated with the business and industrial world, with key figures in the nation's economy and politics, and with masses of infinitely detailed factual material. The poet who only two years before had despaired of finding answers to the mystery behind the universe was required to write lucid reports on such topics as the building boom in skyscrapers, unemployment relief, and the strange case of Ivar Kreuger.

The startling difference between MacLeish's writing in Europe and his writing in America might be illustrated by the utter despair expressed in the final lines of *The Hamlet of A. MacLeish* (1928) which read, *"Thou wouldst not think / How ill all's here about my heart!"* and the gastronomical enthusiasm of lines from his first piece in *Fortune*, March, 1930, "and Apple Pie": "Each weighs a rough three pounds. A knife will cut it. Three divisions will reduce it to six appropriate triangles. Each triangle will emit a faint warm smell of cinnamon and nutmeg. Subdivided with a four-pronged fork and tasted, the mouth remembers apples. Cheese consorts with it. Coffee leaves it sweet."[1] In the June, 1930, issue were MacLeish articles on the banker, Albert Henry Wiggins, and on the "Five Who Found Eternal Youth"—among them the Old Dutch Cleanser Girl, the Uneeda Biscuit Boy, the Holeproof Girl, the Arrow Collar Man. In the July issue began the first of six articles on Skyscrapers. The poet had to give form to a mass of minutely detailed material. The man who had written, "A poem should not mean / But be" was explaining construction problems in a very congested district: "Consequently the foundations of the new building will go down beside the foundations of existing buildings, which will have to be shored in process, and against the margins of streets which must not only be supported but so supported that the channels of communication—water supply, gas supply, electricity, sewage disposal and signals—shall not even momentarily be interrupted."[2]

In the year 1931 and after, he was writing about corporation lawyers, the Harrimans, labor, Samuel Insull II, the Rivera frescoes; he was drafting nine or more articles on housing, on "Wonder Boys in Washington," charity, inflation, and other topics that would broaden his knowledge of America. His writing required that he become knowledgeable in the problems, classes of people, and personalities involved in the Great Depression. His work demanded that he become an observer, that he give some meaning to masses of detailed material. He also had to deal with controversial subjects. In the article, "The Case Against Roosevelt," published in the December 1935, issue, he discussed the emotional support and violent antipathy that surrounded Franklin D. Roosevelt just before the 1936 election. The antagonism was more personal than theoretical. The article is interesting not only for its insight into the public temper of the time but for the rhetorical, discursive style that MacLeish was developing. The balance of clauses and the repetitions of words, a style that became more and more characteristic of some of his poems, can be illustrated by one typical sentence: "The reason for the personal hostility of business toward the President is, in other words, the fact that the President has been personal in his relations to business and that those whom the President's government have offended have felt themselves offended by the President in person."[3]

During the early 1930's MacLeish was also contributing articles on technology and the machine, on the leftist writers, on the nature and the role of poetry in society to such magazines as *The Saturday Review of Literature, The New Republic, The Nation,* and *Poetry, A Magazine of Verse.*

II New Found Land (1930)

New Found Land, the first book of poems published after his return to America, revealed a poet torn between the old world and the new—a nostalgia for what he had left, mixed feelings about what it was to be an American, and a longing to find a myth significant to his own land. The volume includes poems of distinction, poems that have been accepted as among the best of our time. Others are obviously addressed to a larger audience than are the previous tightly designed, introspective lyrics; and they are, consequently, more loosely constructed, the imagery less densely stated.

Among the poems reminiscing of the old world is "Memory Green" which records emotions associated with certain places—"dusk along the Friedrichstrasse" or "Paris on the windy quay" and which conveys the nostalgia of cherished memories:

> You will not understand why suddenly sweetness
> Fills in your heart nor the tears come to your eyes:

"Cinema of a Man" gives in a series of impressions—of associations, pictures, moods, people, and places—a portrait of a man whose heart belongs to two worlds. The juxtaposition of images without connectives, though characteristic of St.-John Perse and of Chinese poetry as well, gives the effect of cumulation rather than tension:

> He walks with Ernest in the streets in Saragossa
> They are drunk their mouths are hard they say qué cosa
> They say the cruel words they hurt each other
> Their elbows touch their shoulders touch their feet go
>   on and on together

The predicament of belonging to the new world but stirred by homesickness for the old is repeated in "American Letter," a poem that suggests why it is a strange thing to be an American:

> This land is my native land. And yet
> I am sick for home for the red roofs and the olives,
> And the foreign words and the smell of the sea fall.

A poem of fluid, descriptive lines and casual detail, it drew both praise and criticism. Morton Zabel referred to the "limp humility" of the poem and feared that poems like "American Letter" might permanently disable "the genius in understatement" found in Streets in the Moon.[4] Alfred Kreymborg called it a marvelous poem. He found in it the rich expression of a sensitive American who loved and hated his native country at the same moment.[5] Llewellyn Jones, apropos of this poem, commented on the "spiritual exile" of Ezra Pound and T. S. Eliot

The Poet's Rediscovery of America

"both of whom have cut that umbilical cord of home connection which Mr. MacLeish has never severed."[6]

The poem "Men," which roused strident comment from the proponents of the constricted style, describes in simple, unpunctuated declarative statements the labor of a pioneer people, buoyed by trust and faith and not harried by philosophical questions. Two typical lines are these: "We planted corn grapes apple-trees rhubarb" and "Our history is grave noble and tragic." MacLeish was accused of being an anti-intellectual on the grounds of poems such as this one. In "Land's End" MacLeish turned from the ancient past of Frazer and Classical cultures he had used in *The Pot of Earth* to the primitives of the Arctic, an ancient people who learned wisdom from the blessings and the rigors of nature. About this time (1931), he wrote that St.-John Perse seemed to him to express most profoundly the world in which men were blindly groping; it was this poet, born in Martinique, who used "the scenes and times of pastoral Asia" to comment on the Western world.[7] The people in "Land's End" are relatively primitive; their speech "the tongue of another country"; and their fruits, proverbs, songs, and festivals the record of another kind of life. The poet seeks to learn from these silent men whose word for "sea" is a word meaning "sorrow" and who have seen "Shapes solid and real."

In some of the poems MacLeish relates the whole question of the nature of poetry to the difficulty of bridging past and present, of finding hints to the wisdom ancient men achieved, and of understanding the signs which they left. Although the images are new, lack of communication—the problem raised in *Einstein* and in *Hamlet* and in a number of shorter poems—still remains. The same hopeless task faces the poet who attempts to praise beautiful women. In " 'Not Marble nor the Guilded Monuments' " MacLeish comments on the empty boast of poets who claim to make beauty immortal:

(What is a dead girl but a shadowy ghost
Or a dead man's voice but a distant and vain affirmation
Like dream words most)

"Tourist Death" develops in multiple images throughout the poem the paradox implied in the title, as if the poet were taking Death on a guided tour and suggesting quite frankly times and places where his presence would seem to be incon-

gruous. A few lines from the center of the poem illustrate the
idea that life and death are paired, are two parts of a whole:

> Life is a haft that has fitted the palms of many,
> Dark as the helved oak,
>> with sweet bitter,
> Browned by numerous hands:
>> Death is the rest of it.

There seems to be a more successful communication between
man and nature in two lyrics, "Immortal Autumn" and "You,
Andrew Marvell," which have won large numbers of enthusiastic
readers. George Dangerfield commented on the "deceptive ease"
to be found in "Immortal Autumn" and called it the "most beautiful single poem of his generation":

> I speak this poem now with grave and level voice
> In praise of autumn, of the far-horn-winding fall.
>
> I praise the flower-barren fields, the clouds, the tall
> Unanswering branches where the wind makes sullen noise.
>
> I praise the fall: it is the human season.
>> Now
> No more the foreign sun does meddle at our earth,
> Enforce the green and bring the fallow land to birth,
> Nor winter yet weigh all with silence the pine bough,
>
> But now in autumn with the black and outcast crows
> Share we the spacious world: the whispering year is gone:
> There is more room to live now: the once secret dawn
> Comes late by daylight and the dark unguarded goes.
>
> Between the mutinous brave burning of the leaves
> And winter's covering of our hearts with his deep snow
> We are alone: there are no evening birds: we know
> The naked moon: the tame stars circle at our eaves.
>
> It is the human season. On this sterile air
> Do words outcarry breath: the sound goes on and on.
> I hear a dead man's cry from autumn long since gone.
>
> I cry to you beyond this bitter air.

"Immortal Autumn" is a poem in praise of man's close kinship
to nature that enables him to see in autumn the human quality
and opens the channels of communication so that the meaning
of human life takes on significance. It is a praise of autumn as

"the human season" between the generative period enforced by "the foreign sun" and death when winter imposes silence. The power of communication seems to carry not only from nature to man and man to man but from men of generations long gone to the ones living now. The perplexities and mysteries of the spring are no longer obscure or secret; alone, exposed, and fully aware, man shares the immensity of the world with "the black and outcast crows," and whatever lies beyond. George Dangerfield commented upon the strength and the single significance of the Anglo-Saxon words, words not made sophisticated by multiple meanings.[8] The lines themselves have the strong rhythmic beat of Anglo-Saxon poetry, and the dignity of the poem is enhanced by the regular rhyme pattern of each stanza.

Central also to "You, Andrew Marvell" is the theme of the brevity of life and the imminence of death. Repeated through the delicately regular quatrains is the juxtaposition of images of the rising sun and the rising night, of morning and the chill of dusk, of the flowering and decay of civilizations named in sequence from East to West—Ectaban, Kermenshah, Palmyra, Sicily, Spain, and, by implication, America.[9] The subtle movement in the poem suggests the relentless passage of time, of life and death, of culmination and decay:

> To feel the always coming on
> The always rising of the night:

The sense of Marvell's "time's winged chariot" is communicated in the continuing movement of the lines. The idea of the imminence of death, stated in the first stanza, is traced through seven unpunctuated stanzas illustrating civilizations which have had their day, the most ancient and farthest to the east, and, in succession, the movement of the cultures toward the west— repeating the movement of the sun and the "climbing shadow"— which had their brief moment before extinction. Even with the last three lines is communicated the relentless, endless movement of time:

> And here face downward in the sun
> To feel how swift how secretly
> The shadow of the night comes on . . .

Morton Zabel deplored the "excessively miscellaneous" content represented in *New Found Land* and discovered a range of influence and indebtedness; to him, the volume represents an amalgam of "Eliot's nervous lucidity, Aiken's tinkling languor, and Robinson's clipped aphorisms."[10] Robert Penn Warren, representing the point of view of New Criticism, regretted the anti-intellectualism to be found in poems like "Land's End."[11]

III   Conquistador (1932)

Between the publication of *New Found Land* (1930) and *Conquistador* (1932), MacLeish wrote "Nevertheless One Debt," an essay in which he stated the poet's position in a changing world. With the growth of an industrialized society, individualism had come to an end, and all men were closely interdependent for their basic needs. Poets were aware of this change. The Romantics expressed it by turning inward upon themselves, away from the world. In a different way, Baudelaire and his successors "turned inward upon nerves and emotions"; and, if they turned outward, it was to imitate "the Singular and the Strange." "The spiritual microcosm of Rimbaud, the intellectual mirrors of Mallarmé, the gazing crystal of Parnasse, the religious doubts and classical escapes of Arnold and the English, are all aspects of the same thing. Poetry was aware of the impending event and refused it."

The change came, MacLeish declared, when poets like Apollinaire and Cendars in France and Pound in England, and later Eliot, looked squarely at the contemporary world, talked about belonging to their own time, and made experiments in language and verse forms. They looked at the present world, but their hearts were elsewhere. MacLeish cited the Eliot poem as proof. " 'The Waste Land' is a poem which sees the contemporary world as the wreckage and scattered ruin of many great and fallen cities, and Eliot's masterpiece, though its influence fell forward into the years which followed its publication, was actually a termination; it was a lament, and a prayer. Nothing could follow it but darkness and silence. Or a new beginning."

Part of the new beginning, MacLeish felt, was that poetry must not only perceive but feel that the race of men is more important than any single man. Instead of man, it is mankind: "common, simple, earth-riding ways of hands and feet and flesh against the enormous mysteries of sun and moon, of time, of disappearance"; not the great, "the brass-voices, but these men, these lives, and now death taking them." Poetry's debt, he concluded, was "an image of mankind in which men can again believe."[12]

It was in the perspective of this statement that MacLeish wrote *Conquistador,* an epic of the conquest and exploitation of Mexico, the long poem that won him a Pulitzer Prize and established his reputation. Based on the historical account given by Bernal Díaz del Castillo, the poem is colored by a firsthand acquaintance with the land and its people.[13] During the winter of 1929 MacLeish, on foot and by mule, followed the route of the conquistadors from Vera Cruz to Mexico City.

The four introductory sections to the fifteen books of the poem itself give certain clues to MacLeish's method. In the Pound-Eliot tradition, the "Dedication" is an epigraph; the lines are taken from Dante, *Inferno,* Canto XXVI, lines 112-13, " 'O frati,' dissi 'che per cento milia / perigli siete guinti all'occidente. . . . ' " which John D. Sinclair translates, " 'O brothers,' I said, 'who through a hundred thousand perils have reached the west. . . .' "[14] "The Prologue" is in the epic tradition; it is the poet's appeal to the dead for insight into and true understanding of the past.

As Odysseus in Hades tried "to force truthful speech" from the shades, so the poet addresses the conquerors—Sandoval, Alvarado, Olíd, Olea, Cortés—and finally elicits the voice of an old man as from a long distance. "Bernal Díaz' Preface to his Book" reiterates that his untutored account is a record of his own and his companions' experiences. He resents the learned Gomara's attention to big names and "beautiful battles" recorded in pompous Latin, just as he resents the bright young men with "the pucker of art on their lips." He scorns the report of Fonseca, Bishop of Burgos, as not comparable to anything he and his comrades experienced. Díaz says repeatedly in his Preface that truth is not to be found in the polite records sent to the Emperor. Díaz protests: "We saw that city on the inland sea"— "We were the first that found that famous country"—"We were the lords of it all. . . ." This eighty-year-old soldier recounts the shock of meeting this primitive people and ruefully expresses the bitter taste of hindsight over not foreknowing the evil that was to follow:

> Well I remember the walls and the rusty taste of the
> New-spilled blood in the air: many among us
> Seeing the priests with their small and arrogant faces:

Seeing the dead boys' breasts and the idols hung with the
Dried shells of the hearts like the husks of cicadas
And their human eyeballs and their painted tongues

Cried out to the Holy Mother of God for it:
And some that stood there bore themselves the stone:
And some were eaten of wild beasts of their bodies:

And none of us all but had his heart foreknown the
Evil to come would have turned from the land then:
But the lives of men are covered and not shown—

Only late to the old at their time's ending
The land shows backward and the way is there:

The fourth introductory section, "The True History of Bernál
Díaz—The Argument," echoes the opening of "The Aeneid":
Arma virumque cano. MacLeish's first line reads, *"Of that
world's conquest and the fortunate wars:"*

This American epic, written as an old soldier's recital of the
first white man's march through the spectacular Mexican
country and through hostile Indian territories to the palace of
Montezuma, retains certain familiar qualities to be found in
the earlier MacLeish: fascination with memory fragments, lyric
descriptions of the land and sea, detailed descriptions of scenes,
delineation of character through dialogue, attention to death
images, the subtle relationships among people. There is loyalty
and self-sacrifice, heroic courage and endurance to be found
among men of both nations; on the negative side, there is petty
self-seeking and treachery. Cortés, Montezuma, and even the
Indian woman, Doña Marina, are heroic figures. There are awful
scenes of massacre that arouse a sense of inherited guilt reminiscent of the torment in the MacLeish *Hamlet.* The poet's
interest was obviously in the lyric and descriptive aspects of the
epic rather than in the narrative one.

Many of the historic figures, many place names, and many
incidents of the original source make their appearance, but
often not too clearly. Scenes that might have been dramatized
are not developed. Many of the historic characters involved in
the Spanish factions and some of the Indian characters who
also represent rival factions, all of whom need to be clearly
identified, are often only casually referred to; their relationships
to other characters and to the situation are left obscure. The
characterization of the central figures, however, is clear.[15]

Cortés first appears as he outwits the jealous Velásquez who would arrest him; he embarks at night, and in the morning taunts his rival:

> "Señor! there are some things in this sinful world
> Best done before they're thought of!"

The eloquent and aristocratic Captain Cortés ate off "a service of sound plate" and wore a "Gilded knot to his shirt and his chain gold." He had "a smile for the troops with the orders" but could be sharp if necessary. When he discovered an abandoned town, and his men disobedient, his rebuke was caustic: "Did you pacify people taking their gold and their chickens?" He restored the stolen property and sent messages to the chiefs. From the friendly Indians he learned of a former expedition and sensed a need for precaution. After eight days of waiting they saw appearing a naked old man, Jeronimo de Aguilar, a one-time priest, who became their interpreter to the Indians.

Book IV apparently describes Cortés' handling of the Velásquez' faction, but the identities are obscure. Cortés founded Vera Cruz, built a gallows and a jail which he gave, along with eloquent words and gold, to the Governor's man: "What a salve is gold to console the mind!" Cortés was made general-in-chief and was granted a fifth of all "gold or goods or discoveries" and words to "enlarge the Emperor's ear." Díaz, his words written for the most part in strong Anglo-Saxon rhythms, expresses admiration for Cortés as his majesty's true servant but bitterness over the small pay and little fame that came to the soldiers who endured hunger, disease, and hardship:

> We that to west now: weirdless: by fates faring
> Follow on star-track: trust have we neither now:
> Traceless this ground: by the grazing deer by the hare crossed:

Díaz fears that their work may be forgotten: "And our deeds be lost in the earth and our times done...."

Book V opens with a condensed recital of Cortés' discovery of the Velásquez traitors and the speedy execution of the leaders—"And Cortés was sick of the night's work:" His speech to these traitors is one of the most distinctive sections of the poem; it characterizes two different views of life. For instance, to quote in part:

This is an undiscovered and dark land:
All this that you say is true: but the words of your
Fear are not true: there is one ship: man her!

Take what you will of the store: a keel's burden:
Spain is east of the seas and the peaceful countries:
The old tongues: the ancient towns: return to them!

He defined the alternatives:

The west is dangerous for thoughtful men:
Eastward is all sure: all as it ought to be:[16]

For the common soldiers the inland march was a continuous adventure in hardship and horror. The wounded cared for themselves with "ravel of torn sleeves ... larded ... from dead men." Peace offerings came from the Indians, "sick of the battle of horses," with gold and girls for the officers. As the Spanish approach their objective, Díaz comments on the drive that impels them onward in spite of suffering, danger, and the unknown, lines again recalling the Anglo-Saxon:

Strange as it is that men: wanderers: wretched:
Deceived often: misled: their way lost: thirsting:
March on in the sun! But so the desire has
Strength over us ...

Of the Indian girls brought to the Spaniards, Doña Marina, mistress to the officers and interpreter for her masters, was most highly honored:

Her face smooth and pleasant to see for an Indian:
Not embarrassed but frank-seeming and simple:

Images of an Indian civilization are frequently introduced: the idols at the Cape of the Women, with "Bellies of stone and stone breasts and their limbs like ..."; frequent references to human sacrifice, as "the smell under the smoke of human blood: / And the bitter odor of death"; or the picture of the Tlaxcalans approaching:

And they came like dogs with their arms down: and their faces

Painted and black and with death's eyes and their breasts
Quilted with cotton and their naked arms:
And the hard hammer of sun on the gold: and their crests like a

Squall of rain across the whitening barley—
We that were mortal and feared death—

In this battle of gunpowder against spears, the Spaniards, far outnumbered, are saved by last-minute reinforcements.

Another scene, the massacre at Cholula because of Indian treachery, culminates in the terrible swift action under Cortés who knew "How they had salt for our flesh in the boiling pot." Some "cried as sheep to be sheared" and confessed, shifting blame on their great king. The awful retribution, described extensively by Díaz, is summed up in one terrible stanza:

Afterward they were blind with the raw blood:
They died slowly with much pain like serpents:
Our hands were lame with the sword when the thing was done . . .

And who are ye to be judge of us . . .?

Montezuma first appears as an image of gold, seated in a golden chair, the straps on his feet golden, the sun image carried before him. His first words are hospitable:

"Malinchi! these are your houses: these your doors:

Yours and your brethren's: you may rest awhile:"

Díaz' description of the city and civilization is out of an old man's halcyon memory: the luxury of long days, clean, sweet-smelling rooms; cool melons; golden naked girls; "sea-doused figs." He also gives a description of the Indian market, excellent in its rich detail of produce, trade, craft and of the physique of men and of girls. And yet, though the land seemed good and the lives rich, it was not so: "And they passed with their cries at dawn and their deep drums: . . . and the boy was slain!

The belly arched to the stone knife: I remember
They sang and were glad as a small child in the sunlight
And they ate the limbs for a feast and the flesh trembled. . . .

Realizing they were fools to think they could live secure in this land, they decide to seize the king. Montezuma tells them their arrival had been prophesied and chides them for fearing death:

for death was dumb
And mute and of lawful life as an herb or as beasts or
Rain is: and savage as stones: and humble:

He promises to follow them quietly, for their steel could hold him. It is this Indian king who makes Cortés realize the mockery of his expedition and the awful consequence of the wars:

> "Had we brought the
> Whore of death to our beds and our house to serve us?
> How should we profit by these deeds? And we thought our
> Ills were done! And the wheel of our luck turned!
> And the toss was tamed to our hands! But it was not so
> But evil fortune and the last and worse and
>
> Great fault of those wars!"

But Cortés was further involved in violence and death when his subordinate, Alvarado, suspecting treachery, slaughtered the natives "that came like wasps in swarms." Cortés cursed him for a violent fool, and returned over lands scarred by their previous wars: "And the towns empty and changed and the cock-wood scattered;" ... "And the dry bleat of the wheels and the silent mountains!" Colua, that once was a city of gardens, was like a charnel house:

> And the place smelled of the doused ash and of hunger and
> Sick men's nights and of death: and the dead were slack in the
> Bloody straw of the earth as a coat is slung:

Cortés with his men was later involved in a battle of survival when Narvaes, whom he had saved, turned traitor and attacked with the combined forces of rival Spaniards and Indians who "came like wolves in the streets." The war-weary Cortés urges his men to action:

> "That the laws of this land were foreign and not ours
> And they laid death as a wafer on their tongues
> And he had no hope of the harvest of that ground:
>
> That men were fools to take the god among them:
> For a man's part is to labor and fear death
> And die in pain and he must and in his hunger:
>
> And the gods were of other lands: nevertheless
> As our will was: and our wisdom: let us do. . . ."

Meanwhile, clad in gold, Montezuma climbed the stair and looked at the war below: "and they fought like dogs in the ditches / Whistling and shrieking ... And all at once there were stones ... and he fell."

His eyes were lewd with the strange smile: and they yelled as
Fiends in Hell and as beasts: and when we thought it
Least for the bitter fighting he was dead:

Cortés' men were trapped—the ways barred, the ditches barred,
the roads held by the enemy: "And nevertheless we had the
choice to take them!..." Cortés' men made an exit at night,
laden with spoils: "Seven hundreds of thousands of *pesos de
oro* / And the pelts of birds and the jade and the painted cotton"
—an exit marked by bloody fighting and the loss of many men.
In revenge the Spaniards laid the city in "a Christian siege"
which lasted ninety-nine days until there was finally "a very
beautiful victory." The conquistadors rebuilt the town on the
model of a Spanish city—barracks, shops "and the church conspicuous." Then came the settlers "like nettles in dry slash: like
beetles," and parceled out the land, jeering at the old soldiers
who had won it for them. Old Díaz remembers what was for
them the new country:

an old man sickened and near death:
And the west is gone now: the west is the ocean sky....

The poem evokes the quality of two civilizations whose re-
ligions focus upon violence and death. Though Cortés wished
to achieve his mission with minimum savagery, his aim was to
subjugate a free people. It is from Montezuma that he learned
the significance of his undertaking: he was the outrider of death.
As old Bernál says at the beginning, if they had known the
"Evil to come would have turned from the land then": The
real heroes in the book are men like the common soldier, Bernál
Díaz, who lived through these wonderful but terrible adventures
and who became aware of the awful tragedy for which he
and his comrades were responsible.

Eda Lou Walton praised "the superb technique and completely
focused point-of-view" of the poem. She thought the story of
Conquistador was a "perfectly handled vivid, clear, excellently
conceived narrative rising to a tremendous climax." She related
the poem to the Eliot tradition: "Here we find the theme of
'The Waste Land' again, for the conquest has come to nothing,
the tale has ended and 'death is the rest of it.' " She saw in the
poem "an account of a magnificent and perished race," the rich
past contrasted to the sterile present, memory being the only
reality. Though it seemed to be a logical development from the

earlier poem, the waste-land theme was in the background. The theme of the intellect and its sterility is dimmed in contrast with "the intense emotional values of actions of an epic scale, with terror, primitive and physical passion, hero-worship, passionate leadership." She implied that nothing else was left to the modern poet obsessed with the idea that modern science and psychology have made life meaningless.[17]

Robert Penn Warren felt that what attracted the poet's imagination was not the narrative nor logic but the lyric quality, "the tone of reverie, the pathos of big deeds swallowed in time." It was "the richness of MacLeish's physical perceptions" that sustained the narrative. He felt that the absence of structure or dramatic sense noticeable in the lyrics was more evident in the longer poems.[18] I. L. Solomon described MacLeish as an "old romantic given to nostalgia," but also as a Classicist, as evidenced in some of the spare, clear lines.[19]

The critic who signed himself "S.F." to the review, "Escape to the Past," berated the poet of *Conquistador* for not following the Marxist party line. He said that the bourgeois intellectual in a decadent middle-class society was forced to seek material from the past, where he "stretches for the heroes and romances, for the values [he] fails to discover in a dying social order." As for the style, he said, "The feminine run-over endings of lines, the hidden assonance and rhyme, the underemphasis subdue the rich active material of the Conquest."[20]

IV Frescoes for Mr. Rockefeller's City (1933)

The Rockefellers' hiring of the distinguished Mexican artist Diego Rivera, an avowed Communist, to paint murals in the main lobby of Radio City was a comedy of errors on the part of well-meaning liberals. They must have known about the mural in Mexico in which Rivera had portrayed John D. Rockefeller, Sr., as a detestable capitalist seated at a table with his friends, all of them eating money. A stormy issue over the mural is a story of cross purposes; when the head of Lenin appeared between the faces of peons, Rivera was paid the contracted $21,000 for work he had not finished, and what he had completed was destroyed. As a postscript to this series of misunderstandings, when the public became so excited over the publicity given the event and the disappearance of all the art forms involved, the nude statues were finally restored.[21]

MacLeish wrote the six poems which make up *Frescoes for Mr. Rockefeller's City* as if he were saying, "Plague on both your houses," as if he were saying that America is bigger and stronger than both the capitalists and the Communists. In the first, "Landscape as a Nude," he describes the land as a beautiful woman:

> She lies on her left side her flank golden:
> Her hair is burned black with the strong sun.
> The scent of her hair is of rain in the dust on her shoulders:
> She has brown breasts and the mouth of no other country.

The strength in this girl makes her unlike "the soft girls naked in vineyards," unlike "the soft naked girls of the English islands." The poet suggests the strength of the country in terms of the west wind—"the long clean wind of the continents"—and in terms of the trees in groves and the grasses which "Run with the plunge of the wind as a wave tumbling"—a line beautiful in its long rhythms and labials. Under her knees is the American corn stubble, not the "green lawn of the Florentines."

"Wild West" calls up an image of Crazy Horse, a lone rider and thinker, and a silent man: "Unless there were children to talk he took no notice." He had been beaten time and time again—his battle with Custer became a legend—and the last time "He had only the meat he had made and of that little." These plains were his country and worth fighting for. The so-called "empire builders," Perham, Cooke, and Morgan, had acquired this land

> forty say fifty millions of acres in gift and
> government grant outright ought to be worth a
> wide price on the Board at two-fifty and . . .

These men never looked at the land; it was only a matter of price to them. It was very different with Crazy Horse:

> His heart would be big with the love he had for that country
> And all the game he had seen and the mares he had ridden
>
> And how it went out from you wide and clean in the sunlight

"Burying Ground by the Ties" brings echoes from the graves of many foreigners who laid the steel, who dug the passes for the Union Pacific and the water holes, who built the gully

spurs and the freight sidings—men who were "Niggers," Por-
tuguese, Magyars, Polacks, Scotsmen, Englishmen, Chinese,
"Squareheads," or Austrians. These, the real empire builders,
who lie buried "Nameless under the ties," their graves marked
by telephone poles, do not ask for pity. They are proud of the
building they have done. By contrast are those generally
advertised as "empire builders":

> There's nothing good in the world but the rich will buy it:
> Everything sticks to the grease of a gold note—
> Even a continent—even a new sky!

"Oil Painting of the Artist as the Artist" is of particular
interest because of the poet's satiric portrait of the pseudo-artist,
"the plump Mr. Pl'f," who is "washing his hands of America."
This ludicrous esthete recalls the image of the nineteenth-
century British poet MacLeish had so aptly parodied.[22] This
"Mr. Pl'f" shuns anything vulgar and large, anything democratic
and belonging to the common people. MacLeish describes this
affected and pretentious artist as follows:

> He thinks of himself as an exile from all this,
> As an émigré from his own time into history
>
> (History being an empty house without owners
> A practical man may get in by the privy stones:
>
> The dead are excellent hosts, they have no objections,
> And once in he can nail the knob on the next one
>
> Living the life of a classic in bad air
> With himself for the Past and his face in the glass for Posterity.)
>
> The Cinquecento is nothing at all like Nome
> Or Natchez or Wounded Knee or the Shenandoah.

In "Empire Builders" the Museum attendant talks about *The
Making of America in Five Panels*: the so-called makers of
America being men like Harriman, Vanderbilt, Morgan, Mellon,
and Barton. "The Original Document under the Panel Paint"
gives a different story; it records the great wealth in land, in
sky, in grasses and animals—all that to Jefferson were promises
for a good life to many people moving west. The "Makers of
America," however, saw land as profit only. The image of the
girl in "Landscape as a Nude" has become an image of the
exhausted whore:

They screwed her scrawny and gaunt with their seven-year
  panics:
They bought her back on their mortgages old-whore cheap:
They fattened their bonds at her breasts till the thin blood ran
  from them.

"Background with Revolutionaries" begins with a chorus that
must have raised the blood pressure of every card-carrying
Communist in the early 1930's:

> And the corn singing Millennium!
> Lenin! Millennium! Lennium!

In rhythms as if he were writing a parody of a work song,
MacLeish spoofs the workmen with good American and English
names who called themselves "Comrade"; he jests at their publication: "*And* The New York Daily Worker *goes a'blowing
over Arkansas.*" He mocks the solemnity of synthetic political
philosophers:

> Even Comrade Grenadine Grilt who had tried since
> August tenth for something to feel strongly in
> Verses—his personal passions having tired.

He mimics the speech in broken English: "Aindt you read in d'
books you are all brudders?" He mimics those who try to squeeze
America into a foreign ideology:

> For Marx has said to us, Workers what do you need?
> And Stalin has said to us, Starvers what do you need?
> You need the Dialectical Materialism!

Interspersed between the stanzas jesting at the solemn and
squint-eyed "revolutionaries" are stanzas suggesting the great
aims and strength of the country which this small group of
theorists were trying to change. The poem—and the book—
closes with lines that express a strong belief in America:

> *She's a tough land under the oak-trees, mister:*
> *It may be she can change the word in the book*
> *As she changes the bone of a man's head in his children:*
> *It may be that the earth and the men remain . . .*
>
> *There is too much sun on the lids of my eyes to be listening.*

The temper of the left-wing critics at the time can be illustrated from one violent review. Michael Gold, a Communist convinced of the political uses of the arts and poetry, saw in these poems the "mystic nationalism" of Hitler and another sign of the fascist mission in "Mr. MacLeish's contempt for Marxists, Jews, and those disturbed intellectuals who recently have taken the road to the political left." He granted that MacLeish might be an "unconscious fascist"; he accused him of putting to use fascist tricks: for instance, chanting the pathos and heroism of labor; contrasting the present with a "golden past" that was only myth. Gold attempted to correct what he considered to be MacLeish's distorted vision. He wrote that the share-croppers, the miners, and the sailors were closer to the democratic revolution than the "white-collar Fascists" from Harvard and Wall Street. He put his faith in the thousands of workers ranging from miners in Kentucky to butchers in Chicago's packing houses, to the lumberjacks and weavers in Oregon and New England, respectively.[23]

William Rose Benét answered Michael Gold by suggesting that his extreme sensitivity to MacLeish's reference to certain kinds of "Comrades" in "Background with Revolutionaries" indicated a kind of soft-mindedness. Benét was sure that what really exasperated Gold was the four lines of one vaudeville stanza written in dialect. He thought that to conclude from those few teasing lines that MacLeish was anti-Semitic was a rather large deduction. He suggested that the poet was merely trying to understand his own country and his own time.[24] Llewellyn Jones thought MacLeish contrasted the real America with "the feverish and sectarian activities" portrayed in the Frescoes.[25]

V Mr. MacLeish Answers the Marxists

"Invocation to the Social Muse," a reply to the left-wing critics published in 1932, has been called a key poem in the poetic career of Archibald MacLeish. His bantering tone contrasts with the heavy seriousness of the Marxists. He addressed his observations to Señora, to Fräulein, to Barinya, "the licensed ladies who follow the armies but not given combat status." Speaking then to Tovarich as one of "us girls" of the original profession, the poet declares that the "kept" lady, pursuing her own interests, consorts with stragglers from either side, always remaining neutral. "It is also strictly forbidden to mix in maneuvers." Notoriety too often leads to sudden death. Life to her is more important than the interests of Mr. Morgan, or of Tovarich either, for that matter. "There is nothing worse for our trade than to be in style." MacLeish then shifts the metaphor to the poet as a man who survives longer if he goes naked, alone, without an army in his bed. He asks how a poet can embrace an army, "Take to one's chamber a million souls," or "conceive in the name of a column of marchers." The very personal and intimate nature of poetry makes joining a cause impossible:

> The things of the poet are done to a man alone
> As the things of love are done—or of death when he hears the
> Step withdraw on the stair and the clock tick only.

The poem closes with the question that might signify MacLeish's belief about the poet's position in society as he felt it to be at that time, October, 1932: "Is it just to demand of us also to bear arms?"

This poem is one of MacLeish's early public statements. It is written for the most part in declarative statements or in questions, at times in an unpunctuated series of substantives, and in the terza rima stanza that MacLeish had adapted for the long poem, *Conquistador*. The jesting tone that pervades the poem is like that of his ridicule of the left-wingers in the *Frescoes*, a series also addressed to the wider audience.

"Invocation to the Social Muse" gave rise to a very lively exchange of poems and letters, both supporting and attacking MacLeish. Several well-known names appear among the contributors: Allen Tate, John Peale Bishop, Seldon Rodman, Rolfe Humphries, and Yvor Winters. The two most contested points were whether poets should bear arms and whether it was fair to call poets whores. Mr. Humphries was amused over the responses of the correspondents, some of whose replies were not commensurate with their indignation. Apropos of the sore point about defining poets, he thought MacLeish had "muffed his metaphor," but he did agree that the artist had to be "kept" in any society. Some of the replies reminded MacLeish that poets throughout history had often been men of affairs.[26]

Fortified by considerable knowledge about the industrial economy which had become part of his working background for

Fortune, MacLeish continued to answer the left-wing critics. In "The Social Cant," published in December, 1932, he said that social critics fumbled the meaning of poetry because they fumbled the meaning of the society in which they lived. They worked in coined phrases like "machine civilization" as the cause of the decay in the economy of the time; they talked of the world's being changed "in a given direction by the mechanization of industry"; they thought of industrialism as static. MacLeish replied that industrialism was not a theory but an organic condition, a phenomenon that had long passed out of human control. He compared the rate of development between 1899 and 1919, with that in the years following. After 1919, a date as important in American history as Appomatox, the increase in the number of machines decreased the number of men employed; from this date was foreseeable a greater number of men than jobs. "The new industrialism of the post-war period moves toward a production increasingly freed from human labor and toward a society in which labor will no longer justify life because there will be, within certain limits, no labor to do." With the spectre of permanent unemployment facing greater numbers, the old idea of work as a religion and a morality no longer prevails. The concepts of work and leisure belong to an earlier time. In an industrial economy consumption becomes a right, not a blessing to be earned.

The poet who follows the Marxist dialectic does not observe his own time but distorts his observation to fit a prescribed, outmoded theory. The true poet in modern times, perceiving what industrial society really is, will find "other ends and justifications" than work, consumption, and leisure; for men must have an orientation in order to live with any sense of meaning.[27] MacLeish continued the argument in "The Poetry of Karl Marx." He repeated the thesis that the poet must soak himself in his own time and not in theories about his time, theories not only foreign but a hundred years old. Only those poets who recognize industrialism as a growing and not as a static phenomenon can understand their time. They would then realize that social injustice is not a class crime but has been bred by conditions of an industrialized society.

The Marxist challenges the poet with the alternative of knowing the world "with an artist's single, and arrogant demand of artistic significance" or of seeing the world through the calculated and partisan interest of a cause. The artist cannot be the propagandist. MacLeish defended the truth of poetry by saying that a major part of knowledge of our lives and of our destiny had come from the intuitive perceptions of great poets. As long as the poet acts as a poet, the sole test of his poem is the test of his art; his politics or his social indignation are not relevant. When the poet becomes the servant of a cause, he must accept preconceptions as to the nature and meaning of life, must reject anything contrary to dogma. He must become a special pleader. If he followed the left wing, he would have to soak himself in a dialectic and a theory of another country and another century, with always the same results—pedantry, academicism, intellectualism—and bad poetry. MacLeish deplored the hysteria of the Marxist critics as well as their intolerance. He likewise regretted the passion for negatives among the revolutionary writers, "spiritual infants" who so hated American democracy that they would exchange it for a dictatorship and a classless society to be gained by the sacrifice of millions.[28]

By contrast to these strange new revolutionary writers who act as though God had chosen them to be final architects before even the bricks had been made, MacLeish cited two writers who were, in his estimation, truly revolutionary. He described Maxim Gorky as "perhaps the first creator of a purely proletarian literature ... at all times an artist." In the area of painting, he compared the "profound authority of the artist" in Cezanne with "the partisan and the interested presentation of a skilled and passionate pleader" in George Grosz.[29] He also recommended Carl Sandburg's *The People Yes* as required reading for the revolutionaries: "Out of the book comes for the first time in our literature the people of America. Whitman's men were Man. Sandburg's are men of this earth." The belief in the people and a concern for the oppressed, as represented by Jefferson and Lincoln, are the revolutionary principles basic to the American tradition.[30]

VI Poems 1924-1933

The first anthology of Archibald MacLeish was *Poems 1924-1933*. In the Preface to this edition, the author denied any personal interest in his own development as poet, but the technical development represented belies his own statement. The volume includes most of the poems already discussed, including *Pot of Earth, The Hamlet of A. MacLeish, Conquistador,* as well as the series entitled *Frescoes for Mr. Rockefeller's City.* Certain poems like *The Happy Marriage* were omitted to the regret of some critics.

Of the new poems included, some are obviously experiments in unusual verse forms. A poem like "De votre bonheur il ne reste que vos photos" begins with the word, "since," and closes with five-beat lines. The poem is built upon three statements, "I have not heard," "I have not seen," and "I have never wakened," bound together by three repetitions of the conjunction "since." In "Seafarer," an important poem because of its significant contrast to the uncertainties expressed in *Einstein,* the poet urges man to learn to walk with "the pitch and fall" of the whirling universe. It is written in two quatrains of iambic tetrameter with three lines introduced by the words, "And learn," as if the poet wished to underscore the conviction expressed. "Voyage" communicates zest for life, a characteristic of the young Ernest Hemingway to whom it is dedicated. Again the technical sophistication is to be noted. It is almost as if the spare, direct style of the novelist is suggested in the strictly patterned verse form—three three-line stanzas, the lines in each one parallel, four, two and five-beat—and strength in the four repetitions of the inverted construction: "Heap we," "Keep we," "Raise we," and "Trade we."

A satiric tone pervades three poems with literary themes. In an elegy to Rimbaud, "Aeterna poetae memoria," MacLeish ironically contrasts the "lovers of verses" with a flea-bitten priest who grants the poet forgiveness, a concièrge who never heard of Rimbaud, and an American dealer in manuscripts who "sold the original ink decree" granting divorce to Verlaine's wife. "Critical Observations," reiterating the line, "Let us await the great American novel!" is an amusing comment on the impossible and polyglot nature of such a hybrid work. In "Sentiments for a Dedication" MacLeish aims his barbs against the academicians and critics. He writes not for "unborn generations" but speaks to his own time; the poem closes with the plea, "O living men, Remember me, Receive me among you." Characteristic of his ridicule of the literati are the vignettes of the literary embalmers: "Professor Phlip in Doctor Phlap's goatee / The usual majority of female metics." By way of contrast, "Epistle to Lèon-Paul Fargue," pays tribute to a fellow poet with whom he feels an affinity. MacLeish expressed this close relationship as an intuitive rapport. The poem is made up of a series of analogies of overcasting shadows, as for instance:

> I know that your poems
> Move on my mind as the hand's shade of the fisherman
> Blackens the brass shine out on the sea pool

"Men of My Century Loved Mozart" returns to the myth of Proteus who, enforced through multiple changes, assumes for a moment his human identity. As "the pure deliberate violence of the sun" made the protean self wince and gasp and struggle for a moment and then plunge once more into the sea and "the grateful dark," just so did strains of Mozart compel the mind for one moment to become human

> And wound in web that must more closely bind
> The more it altered from itself, would keep
> One moment in that bond its perfect kind—
>
> Never, when we would question it, but shone
> Through breaking cordage silver and the god was gone.

The power of art to give to man the experience of being completely human is a power which is too tense for long duration and too compelling for any extended human endurance. It is also an experience to be understood by as nearly complete an emotional response as a human being is capable. It is intense and momentary. It cannot be described in intellectual terms, nor analyzed later. The poem, appropriate to Mozart's classical form, is written in a series of formal seven-line stanzas, in rhyme patterns with the last two lines of each stanza a couplet.

Several of the poems are elegiac in theme and very much alike in form. The deep organ notes of the sonnet, "The Revenant," can be illustrated by the slow movement of the first line: "O too dull brain, O unperceiving nerves." In "Lines for an Interment," a tribute to his brother killed in Belgium fifteen years before, the poet speaks in bitter irony of the current attitudes toward the men who died in World War I. For the 1930's the war was an excuse for noisy celebration or a theme for recantation: the words "courage," "honor," and "death" appeared to have been unfortunate, the real causes being economic.

> Now that we understand we judge without bias:
> We feel of course for those who had to die:

Women have written us novels of great passion
Proving the useless death of the dead was a tragedy.

Bitter enmities erased, the horrors of war explained away and forgotten, the survivors return to the Midi and to Bavarian beer; and men like his brother "can rest now in the rain in the Belgian meadow—"

Another sonnet, "Pony Rock," written as a memorial to a friend, intimates a kind of immortality in the way other men look at and love the hills he knew; as if coming upon a word that calls back joy or a "crazy sweetness," they "Will stare at the black print till the page is blurred." "Nat Bacon's Bones" and "Galán," tributes to men killed for their beliefs, their graves and names erased, are poems in formal quatrains with the rhythmic quality of old ballads.

"Elpenor," originally titled "1933," was the Phi Beta Kappa poem read at Harvard that year. William Rose Benét called it a major poem and related it to the book-burning episode in Berlin on March 10, 1933.[31] Written only a few months after "Invocation to the Social Muse," it by no means conveys the same certainty of the role that the poet should play in society. The shocking turn of events in Germany which threatened to destroy civilization were too serious to permit the intellectual and the artist to go his lonely, arrogant way. Events made the old theory of esthetics inadequate. It would seem that at this time MacLeish broke with the Eliot tradition that focused upon the past and cast his choice with the contemporary world.

The poem is a modern retelling of the ancient myth in which Odysseus goes to the House of Hades to learn how to proceed on his way home. The modern Odysseus speaking to Elpenor, the Homeric character who had fallen to his death in a drunken stupor, comments on the personalities he sees in Hell. MacLeish, describing the mentality of the Germans who became Nazis, anticipates the vignettes he was to write in "The German Girls! The German Girls!":

And the redblooded, twofisted, gogetting,
He-ghosts froghonking wretchedly,

And from cairns and from creaks and from rock piles,
And out of the holes of foxes,

Fools booming like oracles,
Philosophers promising more

And worse to come of it yet
And proving it out of the textbooks.

These leaders, though in Hell, are still "Ranting orations from balconies," peddling a reactionary doctrine palatable to those who prefer above all else a comfortable life.

Elpenor—ironically, the name in Greek describes a man who believes his future does not depend on his own choosing to act—jeers at Odysseus' asking the way back. With frequent repetitions of the phrase, "the way back," Elpenor implies that the way back is only the return to an old order of life, a kind of serfdom which man has outgrown with the centuries. Elpenor urges Odysseus to take the way onward, to begin again, to take to the open sea, to cast his lot with the hard choice of freedom rather than domestic comfort and domination by the brutish ruler, to depend on himself "In spite of gods and the prophecy!" The alternatives suggested in these lines are key to the choice that MacLeish was to develop over and over again in his polemical articles on fascism in the 1940's and on communism in the 1950's.

The ten-year record represented in the anthology, *Poetry 1924-1933*, shows the development of a poet who had mastered a poetic technique in several forms, from the tightly designed personal lyrics to the more loosely constructed poems written for a wider audience. The tone ranges from delicate insight into personal relationships, to the elegiac mood, to the sense of loss from man's spiritual limitations, to the broad jesting of the satirical poems. The volume also shows the range from the deep soul-searching of the "expatriate" years to the strong sense of direction and mission represented in poems of the early 1930's.

VII *The Critical Evaluations*

A number of critical statements about *Poems 1924-1933* are genuine assessments of the poet's achievements up to that time. Alfred Kreymborg called the volume "a beautiful book" which summarizes the post-war period, the "expatriate" movement. He described it as a closing chapter, a farewell. He praised MacLeish as a superb craftsman, gave highest praise to the pictorial and musical qualities of the verse. He noted the mood and themes which won for MacLeish a growing audience, and he was certain that his best work would "survive contemporary arguments."[32] Robert Penn Warren, converted to the lyrics of Donne and the seventeenth-century poets and perhaps not sympathetic with the theory of poetry as orchestration, did not respond to the lyric pattern MacLeish had forged. He said that the poet recorded stimuli but showed "no power to dominate them, to organize them as communication for anything more than the simple mood." He thought he found a sameness in the pattern: a question, a deft catalogue of stimuli, a concluding inarticulate cry. He felt that any rearrangement of lines or stanzas, except for the last, in poems like "Cinema of a Man," "Land's End," "American Letter," among others, would not destroy the effect.[33]

Eda Lou Walton wrote that MacLeish was a lyric poet, not a satirist nor a social theorist. Because he was not a controversialist, "his art has been injured by his compulsion to fight." MacLeish, she thought, speaking to his own generation, summed up its feeling: his "strongest passion is a sense of irrevocable loss." She believed that all the poets of *The Waste Land* school have been crippled: with superb technique they have developed an "amazing precocity in sensations of suffering and defeat, a passionate life in letters." What was needed, she believed, was a Gerard Manley Hopkins with his richer powers of association in language, more exactness and directness of expression, "the poet who is a whole man and not a cripple sensually or intellectually."[34]

Conrad Aiken thought that MacLeish spoke first with one voice and then with another: sometimes like Eliot in "Gerontian," more often like Pound of the "Cantos" or "Cathay." He cited *Einstein* and "You, Andrew Marvell" as "among the finest poems of our generation," both having behind them the "tough thinking" that promised so much. He preferred them to the "extraordinary skillfull pastiche of evasions" to be found in poems like *The Pot of Earth, Hamlet,* and *Conquistador.* He found a too frequent repetition of "the nostalgic, the note of self-pity, the 'pathos of distance'"—themes insufficient for "a poet to make us all envious."[35]

Morton Zabel found in *Poems 1924-1933* much fine verse and a poet who had dedicated himself to his craft and to his personal predicament. He saw in MacLeish's struggles a typical experience: a duty to devise a spiritual doctrine when inherited belief no longer fit the needs of the times, and an acceptance of an esthetic point-of-view before he had discovered his own moral and theoretical material. Commenting on the exodus to Paris of 1918-29 as a kind of aberration, he noted that the experience afforded a "poetic discipline" for MacLeish but that the purely esthetic style of poetry of these Paris years was a denial of his own character and of his sense of responsibility. This conflict, Zabel believed, accounted for MacLeish's adopting literary attitudes typical of the 1920's: the elegiac and the hard-boiled. A sensitive and skilled craftsman, MacLeish had to solve a personal problem—whether to surrender his own intelligence to "the unconscious life of nature and the universe" and to write in the abstractions of *Hamlet* and *Einstein,* or to resist this surrender and write in more personal terms.[36]

R. P. Blackmur felt that MacLeish, in searching for a soul, had confused the concept of soul as expressed and found in others' poetry with his own personal need for self-expression. The long poems, brilliant in imagery and in verbal overtones, lacked form and "plot." This critic believed some of the confusion could be that of any man "not committed to an authoritarian way of life": some, from the poet's use of Pound's and Eliot's "apparatus" —material, habits of thought, rhythm—without making them his own. He also felt that MacLeish lacks Pound's "enormous and inconsequential ragbag of a mind," and Eliot's driving, "connecting" Christianity.[37]

C. G. Poore found *Poems 1924-1933* a distinctive volume. He commented rather fully about the controversy that had surrounded MacLeish:

Many sanguinary rows rage around his head. He is vulnerable to the perpetual rediscovery that he has lived in the same age as Ezra Pound and T. S. Eliot without failing to be enriched by them. One of the great scholastic tussels of our day—man versus machines—finds him tilting hotly at dynamos. He waves red sanguinary rags at the Reds. Half the poets around him have been stirred to dissect him in the public prints, which should be recognition and honor enough for any poet, whatever the verdicts. . . .

The great thing about MacLeish is that he outlives one style— or period—after another, and manages to write first-rate poetry in each. That is why so much of the criticism leveled against him is true, and yet, because of the fact that he is constantly making it have the air of posthumous advice (by meantime moving on to new meters and new themes), profoundly irrelevant. It takes something like a renaissance canon of criticism to encompass the mordant introspection of "The Hamlet of A. MacLeish," the full-throated chant of "Conquistador," the observed but not wholly realized anguish of "The Pot of Earth," the racy lampooning of "Frescoes for Mr. Rockefeller's City," and all the shorter poems that also are in this ten-year harvest.[38]

CHAPTER 4

Public Speech

I

IN HIS LITERARY QUARRELS with the Marxist critics, MacLeish repeatedly asserted that the true poet observes the world; and, from his intuitive understanding of what he sees and feels, he writes his poems. If he becomes a special pleader, he betrays his art.

In "Public Speech and Private Speech in Poetry" (1938) he developed more fully an idea suggested in "Nevertheless One Debt" (1931) of the difference between the British nineteenth-century poetry and the revolutionary poetry of Yeats, Pound, and Eliot. The British poet was "the private speaker, the whisperer to the heart, the unworldly romantic, the quaint Bohemian, the understander of women, the young man with the girl's eyes." He is a ridiculous figure, said MacLeish, to follow the tradition of Milton and Dante; he is not capable of understanding stockbrokers, coalpits, and starving children. The poetry of Greece and Rome, of Dante, Chaucer, Shakespeare, Milton, Dryden, and even of Pope was public speech. These poets knew "the meaning of their times better than the men who did not write could know them." Like all the best poets, they were at home in the world.

MacLeish described the poetry of Yeats, Eliot, and Pound as the breaking of the tea-cup china of *The Idylls of the King*. They returned poetry to the world and the poet "to a position of common responsibility among the men and women of his time." Yeats, whom he described as "the best of modern poets," lived without any mannerism of self-conscious genius, without inventing differences between himself and other men: "He is quite simply a man who is a poet." His later poetry "is the first poetry in generations which can cast a shadow in the sun of actual things—men's lives, men's wills, men's future. With Yeats, poetry becomes an engine capable of employing all the mind, all the knowledge, all the strength." But Yeats was not willing to follow through "where the poetic revolution crosses the revolution in the social and political and economic structure of the post-war world." Other poets had to make a difficult choice, "to resign either from their age or from their art. Many of them, unable to comprehend within a rhetorical art a generation of violence and tragedy and menace, have been driven either out of their art into silence or out of their age into dreams." Taking a cue from Thomas Mann that for our time "the destiny of man presents its meanings in political terms," MacLeish described the revolutionary poetry of Yeats and Pound and Eliot as "a transition towards a poetry capable of accepting a political and revolutionary era upon its own terms... a transition capable of restoring a poetry of public speech."[1]

In a second essay, "Poetry and the Public World" (1939), MacLeish continued the discussion but in terms of the nature of poetry. Poetry, he said, is neither more than an art—truth, beauty, goodness—nor is it less than an art: another way of writing. Neither is it "simply an art." Poetry is not *a* way, but *the* way in which something is written: "Art is a method of dealing with our experience of this world, which makes that experience, *as* experience, recognizable to the spirit." It is not the means of extracting truths, nor for communicating information. It is not a device for seeing within ourselves, nor an aid to help us in self-understanding: "Art is an organization of experience in terms of experience, the purpose of which is the recognition of experience.... The truth of a work of art is the truth of its organization. It has no other truth."

For this reason any experience whatsoever "may be brought to the labor of art." There is no limit to the kinds of material proper to poetry:

> "It may be any experience whatever which requires for its intensity the intensity of the poetic line, the shock of the poetic association, the compression of the poetic statement, the incantation of the poetic word. It may be any experience of which the intensity is so great that only a corresponding intensity of order can give it shape, as the tension of flight gives form and beauty to the beating of wings.
> Poetry is to violent emotion what the crystal is to the condensing salt or the equation to laborious thinking—release, identity, and rest.... Only poetry can present the closest and therefore

least visible experiences of man in such form that they, reading, may say: "Yes... Yes... It is like that.... That is what it is truly like."

When Thomas Mann wrote *Reflections of a Non-Political Man* (1918), he illustrated the idea that for a man of culture public and private worlds are separate. After his flight from Germany in 1933 he wrote that "'the political and the social are parts of the human: they belong to the totality of human problems and must be drawn into the whole.'" In the late 1930's MacLeish likewise expressed the belief that, in a revolutionary time such as the mid-twentieth-century, political events have made every single man a part of what happens in every country. Every individual in the modern world is involved in "experiences of intense and personal emotion," such as poetry alone can make recognizable. However, very few poets have attempted "to give poetic order to the political experience of our time." It seemed incredible that "no contemporary poet has yet presented to us, in the personal and yet universal terms of poetry, our generation's experiences of the political world." Not even Yeats did what poetry in other periods had done. There has been no *Hamlet* to "reduce to poetic order" and make recognizable the political world of our time.

MacLeish credited this failure to the continued imitation of Pound and Eliot and other so-called modern poetry that reflected the French of Verlaine and Laforgue; all of this poetry, he thought, belongs before World War I. The imitators have continued the attitudes and idioms after the "relevance has vanished." Pound and Eliot represent a poetry of literary revolt rather than a poetry of rebuilding. The poet writing honestly of our time "requires the responsible and dangerous language of acceptance and belief, a language not possible in poetry of revolt. Only when the poetry of literary revolt had written itself out would contemporary poetry "reduce to the order of recognition, the public-private world in which we live."[2]

These essays were written after the publication of the volume of poetry, *Public Speech* (1936), and after the writing of three short plays between 1936 and 1939. MacLeish had involved himself more completely in the public world and had made his poetry express the meaning of our time in political terms. The journalistic writing begun with the early contributions to various magazines and the editorial responsibilities of *Fortune* continued through the decade and were collected and published in *Housing America* (1932), *A Time to Speak* (1941), and *A Time to Act* (1942).

II   Public Speech

This volume of poems, *Public Speech* (1936), marks the beginning of the role that Archibald MacLeish was to play with increasing dedication and articulateness: that of spokesman for American democracy. In 1933 in *Elpenor* he had described the "froghonking" Nazis and what their domination foreshadowed. In the years following, he had watched the increasing power of the brutish element and had realized what this meant for courageous intellectuals like Thomas Mann. MacLeish's awareness of dangerous times is reflected in much of the poetry in this volume. Many of the poems are different from the delicate lyrics of the earlier volumes because they are directed to a larger audience, a public one. Because of this different perspective, many of the straightforward lines are often a bit discursive and have the quality of public speech. Nevertheless, in this same volume is also included the kind of lyric that readers had come to expect of MacLeish, delicately and perceptively stated, such as the sequence, "Woman on the Stair."

The first poem, "Pole Star," gives a definition of humanitarian love. In a delicate pattern of repetitions, the star is described as "motionless," of "ancient sureness," and again as "star's changelessness, not changing," the focus of "wandering men," of the "waylost, the wanderers," for whom "every guide-mark of the mind"—liberty, pride, hope—has vanished. "Love's star will not." It is the kind of love that has seen a man's eyes "Bloody from the slugger's blows / Or heard the cold child cry for hunger—," that has listened to proclamations of the virtuous who would "murder starve and burn" to make a paradise on earth. It is "Love like hatred and as bright." Written in twelve continuing quatrains of trochaic tetrameters, it is made up of two units: the first, a descriptive statement; the second, a definition.

Three of the poems, written in terza rima, in rhythmic lines reminiscent of *Conquistador,* are poetic speeches which illustrate the poet's commitment to brotherhood, to human love, and to the American dream rather than to a foreign ideology. Addressed to all kinds of workers on all kinds of jobs, the poems seem to be directed to all Americans, some of them like the real empire builders of *Frescoes*. They appear to have been written for the common reader rather than the intelligentsia. The first, "Speech to those who say Comrade," defines what really constitutes brother-hood: bonds formed by those who have shared fear, hunger, indignity, and common associations of youth:

> A wave of men who having the same years
> Have in common the same dead and the changes.
>
> The solitary and unshared experience
> Dies of itself like the violations of love
> Or lives on as the dead live eerily:

Those who are "born brothers" are the "puddlers" in foundries, have ridden the rivers on logs, have fought city police, are veterans of the same ships. It is the shared experience, the shared danger that counts: "Brotherhood! No word said can make you brothers!"

The second, "Speech to the Detractors," is praise of the common man who values "wasteless things"; the excellence of the earth and of art, of honor; "the unnamed motherless peoples" who bring wreaths but do not wear them:

> Because the common face, the anonymous figure,
> The nameless and mortal man,
> Is our time's birth to bear and to be big with—

Monuments raised to heroic figures are soon erased by the "ignorant and rabble rain." Envious men hated T. E. Lawrence when he died, "Fearing there might have lived / A man really noble, really superior." Nobility rests with those large-minded common men who bestow honor. When men leave praise un-spoken, when they cheat "worth of wonder," they are themselves plundered. The third "Speech to a Crowd," is addressed to the perennial "awaiters of messages" whether from "under a child's crib in a manger," or by oracles beneath the transoms, or from Miss Lonely-Hearts. It is addressed to all men who have dreamed of a better world in some future time, who trust to what they read rather than to what experience has taught them. "Waiting for messages out of the dark you were poor. / The world was always yours: you would not take it."

"The German Girls! The German Girls!" is a bitterly satiric characterization of Nazi storm troopers, mindless middle-class primitives obsessed with sex and killing. The poem is built on a frequent and chilling question to the women who tardily remembered it was they who allowed themselves to become whores: "*Are you familiar with the mounted men?*" Their answer creates a vignette of the fascist mind and character:

Are you familiar with the mounted men
The cavalry lot with the hot leap at the fences,
Smellers of horse-sweat, swingers of polished boots,
Leather crotch to the britches, brave looters,
Lope over flower beds, wheel on the well-kept lawn,
Force your knees in the negligée under the awning,
Bold boys with a blouse, insolent handlers,
Bring you the feel again, bring you the German man:
Bring you the blood to the breasts and the bride's look on you—
Laughter fumbling at the clumsy hooks.

The poem closes with the bitter self-accusation of women who realize the role they played in this orgy of sex and death: "Only by women's tenderness can come / The midnight volley and the prison drum-beat!"

In "'Dover Beach'—A Note to that Poem" MacLeish gives a positive answer to the pessimism of Matthew Arnold whose memorable lines recall the disillusionment over lost religious values:

But now I only hear
Its melancholy, long, withdrawing roar,
Retreating, to the breath
Of night-wind, down the vast edges dreer—

MacLeish writes from the point of view of a man who has reached forty, who is willing to let the sea's force and violence surge over younger men, and who recognizes that "the ebb has its own beauty," and that it also

has its lovely uses—
It's the outward wave that spills the inward forward
Tripping the proud piled mute virginal
Mountain of water in wallowing welter of light and
Sound enough—thunder for miles back. It's a find and a
Wild smother to vanish in: pulling down—
Tripping with outward ebb the urgent inward.

The poet looks ahead with the optimistic view that allows the young man to take over; his own generation did its work. The interdependence of the two generations and the willingness to let the younger men assume their active role are stated in terms of the roaring surf and the withdrawing waters of the sea. This effective poem illustrates MacLeish's achievement of a musical line and his willingness to make a frank personal statement.

The sequence of poems entitled "The Woman on the Stair" returns to the intuitive, suggestive insights into the personal feelings and relationships between man and woman. There is a variety of verse patterns in the ten poems, some in terza rima, some in quatrain, some in an irregular two-line stanza. This series of lyrics which touch upon subtle human relationships, all of them in beautifully stated musical lines, represents a style of poetry that, in a time when obscurity and private symbolism have been the vogue, has been somewhat slighted.

The image of barrenness and of rejection of love which appear in "The White Poem" recalls comparable images in the earlier *Pot of Earth*: "Over were three gulls / And your mouth like salt and you hated me." In "The Absence," separation is stated in terms of starvation and thirst—"No hunger was ever sharp as this hunger—" This poem is a fluid statement in three terza-rima stanzas with a concluding fourth, its last line a sharp image of absence: "Continuing the night out by the iron tongues." The third poem, "The Treachery," is in a patterned series of two irregular-lined stanzas with a repetition of concession clauses beginning with the word "although." The analogy is made between the candle flame standing straight when protected against the wind by the curved hands and "the desperate heart's inexplicable calm" against nagging doubts.

"The Quarrel"—in rhymed quatrains—is a series of denials about charges of infidelity. "The Reconciliation," again in terza-rima stanzas but each one a separate unit, comments on the restoration which time has brought, if only in part. The cleavage wrought by insidious doubt is ironically stated in lines such as these: "Between this night and that there is no human distance," and again, "And yet the stars most far apart are not more distant." The sixth poem, "The Second Love," is written in seven terza-rima units. The idea is expressed that love's adulation has a separateness both for those who do not love as those who do: "They stare / Each in the other's face like those who feed / Delight in mirrors:" In "Room by the River" the ironic delusion about the permanence of love is projected by the analogy of sexual union and by the recurring rush of the surf.

The seventh poem, "The Remembrance," is a studied exercise in repetitions of the words "forget" and "forgotten," of combinations with the word "light"—and the delicate quality of memory: "Night is never alone, it remembers." The ninth, "The Late Meeting," is a deceptively simple but subtle comment on one of the closest of human relationships:

> Too cold too windy and too dark
> The autumn withholds the bees
> And bold among the door-yard trees
> The crow cries, the wild foxes bark.
>
> Day alters, seasons alter, we
> Walking the wet rut alter too:
> The fault of strangeness is with you:
> Strangeness is the fault in me.
>
> We know each other, not the friend
> Each for the other's love once made:
> We know the cold, and are afraid
> Of new years, now the year will end.

In the final poem, "The Release," the poet in images of time and memory records experience of a relationship that has come to an end—"Time's past is still: / Time's stillness has taken you."

III *Poetic Drama for Radio*

In 1935 MacLeish wrote that there was no real theater in America because playwrights had only written entertainment for theatergoers. Real theater, and for MacLeish that meant poetic drama, should attempt to get at the "underlying reality" behind the outside surface of men's lives. Eugene O'Neill, often described as a poetic dramatist, only made comments and delivered explanations from the outside. Maxwell Anderson's *Winterset* (1935), not distinctive as poetic drama, nevertheless did grapple with the mentality and central issues of its time. MacLeish felt that the tradition of realism had prevented drama from fulfilling its role. Realistic drama was only description. Poetic drama, on the other hand, was discovery. The poet of the theater, observing the chaotic events of his time, must seek the underlying meaning and must project an image that captures the significance of the multifaceted world in which he lives.

MacLeish believed that poetic drama went to the heart of

what theater should be: "Its essence is precision, but precision of the emotion, not the mind. Its quality is to illumine from within, not to describe from without. Its language is not communication, but experience."[3] MacLeish himself turned to poetic drama to explore the "underlying reality" beneath the surface of the late 1930's. The three short plays—*Panic, The Fall of the City,* and *Air Raid*—represent the poet's desire to deal with major themes that would satisfy his own concept of poetic drama for the radio and would be concrete and vivid enough to reach a large audience.

IV Panic (1936)

In the Preface to *Panic* MacLeish described his search for a verse form that would catch the rhythms of contemporary speech. Elizabethan blank verse was appropriate to a deliberate people but not to the Americans whose speech "is a language of accents," the rhythms nervous and excited. For the principal scenes in his play, for those involving bankers, the lawyers, and the radicals, he adopted "a line of five accents but unlimited syllables." For the scenes spoken by the street voices he "varied the form by using a three-beat line constructed like the five-beat line of the body of the poem."

Panic is set in New York, February, 1933, at the peak of the financial crisis. Two concurrent scenes are represented: the office of the financier McGafferty by a platform where the ticker tape communicates the mood of crisis, and the street where the representative crowd reads the news bulletin across the top of the building. The horror of impending financial panic and the fear of an unknown enemy are communicated on both levels. On the street a woman expresses the paradox of the times:

> A land of great wealth and the
> Old hungry: the young
> Starving—but not with hunger.
> None have beheld this enemy.
> What arms can defend the
> Evening—the night hours—
> When fear: faceless: devours us?

McGafferty asks, "What's done it? / Who's behind it?" The lesser millionaires, thinking McGafferty secure, ask how anyone fights fog. Not only do the street people, facing hunger, a painful old age and miserable death, look to McGafferty for help but the bankers also look to him for direction. At first he proposes a bold unified action. The Blind Man, spokesman for the unemployed who invade the office, speaks for the bankers as well: the two classes are but two parts of the whole problem. Of the unemployed, he says:

> Greatness they have forgotten and pride and the envy of
> Nobler lives than their own and the service of honor.
> To suffer for no gain: to invite death in the
> Hope only of good is a fool's fate to them.

To the bankers he says:

> You yourselves in your own minds will make the
> Fate that murders you. The bursting seed of
> Death is rotting ripe beneath your tongues!

When the Blind Man's fingers grope for and touch McGafferty's face, there is almost a dead stillness. Only the insistent beat of the ticker tape breaks the silence. To McGafferty's sneering inquiry about the end of the prophecy, the Blind Man says that the desire for death is ripening in the banker's own mind. At first when the lesser bankers choose to act, each one for himself, McGafferty vows to stay and fight alone; but he is soon obsessed with the Blind Man's prophecy. He struggles to maintain his position as strong man; unaware that he is describing himself, he expresses contempt for the revolutionaries as "sick souls," as men who would be "rid of the hard choice," who seek "a safe life with dignity."

The second half of the play portrays the rapid disintegration of the world's wealthiest man. The entrance of McGafferty's well-dressed "pink punk," Ione, prevents him from making a decision, induces him to take precautionary half measures. The voices of the street people reflect the state of affairs—"crash crisis increasing"—"last hope lost"—"doomers of earth"—images suggesting the theme of an old order fallen. In a scene long in proportion to the earlier part of the play the banker and his mistress discuss their love affair and the woman's position when the money is gone. The sound of the ticker tape, increasingly loud and rapid, finally alerts McGafferty to the discovery that a moratorium has been declared. The shocked people—"drifting ghosts"—turn against the financiers and look for another strong leader:

> The world's to the nameless man who'll
> Brag in the sun and withstand it and
> Stiffen our hearts that drift like
> Fog on a wave's lifting
> Following every current!

The news of Shelton's suicide—"Bull's face and the hands like fists"—incapacitates McGafferty and prevents him from following his subordinate's urgent plan to act quickly; he placidly waits for the disaster, "Standing as steers would to the butcher's maul." As a last resort he refuses the final indignity, public confession, by taking his own life. The play closes on the enigmatic lines

> The trumpet of
> Time in our ears and the brazen and
> Breaking shout of our days!

> Man's fate is a drum!

Implied in the play is a theme to which MacLeish was to return frequently. Both rich and poor, softened by comfort and by varying degrees of property and wealth, would sell out their individual freedom in order to save material comforts. They would rely on authority rather than upon the truth of their own experience.[4]

There are interesting records about three audiences which attended this play. At the first were the reviewers and invited guests; at the second, "the rich"; and, at the third, partly a "society" audience, and partly second-string critics, as well as readers of *The New Theatre* and *The New Masses.* Joseph Wood Krutch reported that the "orthodox radicals" regarded MacLeish with suspicion and accused him of "doctrinal ambiguities." He thought the play more classic than revolutionary and the playwright more poet than teacher.[5] Ashley Dukes, commenting on the compactness of the material into ninety minutes of playing time, called the play a "mignificent fragment."[6]

V The Fall of the City (1937)

In his foreword to *The Fall of the City* MacLeish described the possibilities of verse drama for radio. He believed that, when there were no distractions, "the word-excited imagination" would overcome many of the difficulties of the theater. "The more packed and allusive the word, the more illuminating its rhythms, the more perfectly is the scene prepared, the more convincingly is the play enacted." In this play he made use of the Announcer whom he described as "the most useful dramatic personage since the Greek Chorus." He saw in radio drama a new medium and was optimistic over the size of the radio audience that would be available for poetic drama.

In *The Fall of the City* MacLeish might have dramatized the famous Franklin Delano Roosevelt warning, "There is nothing to fear but fear itself." It is a play about a city, demoralized by terror, which passively chooses death rather than a fight for its life. In form, the play resembles a news broadcast in which an Announcer gives an on-the-scene account of the approach of a strong man, dispassionately describes events and moods, and interprets them. Various points of view are represented by the first and by the second Messenger, by an Orator, by the Priest, and by an Aged General. The entrance of the Conqueror is described. The dramatic tension derives from the timing of the episodes and from the frustrating efforts of leaders to direct great masses of people who prefer slavery to freedom. It is a symbolic representation of the disintegration of people who exchange the challenge of freedom and individual choice for the certainty and "comfort" of authoritarian rule.

The Voice of the Studio Director sets the scene by describing a city gripped with terror, waiting for catastrophe. The Announcer describes the plaza and the town, with the crowds waiting for an omen from the tomb. At twelve o'clock the Voice of the Dead Woman speaks the prophecy:

> The city of masterless men
> Will take a master.
> There will be shouting then;
> Blood after!

The Announcer describes the crowd as "milling around us like cattle that smell death." The First Messenger describes what has happened to other towns and people defeated by the Conqueror:

> Shame is his people.
> Lickers of spittle
> Their lives are unspeakable:
> Their dying indecent.

He tries to warn the people but they reject the truth of his firsthand observation. Passive and without courage, they prefer to place their trust in the ministers, the old men. They get their answer from the Orator who rejects force as a treacherous weapon and advocates non-resistance: "Weakness conquers!" He urges the crowd to let the strong man come because, he says, words win. The crowd, without thinking, accepts his advice; even the old men are dancing. "A great speech! really great!" glibly comments the Announcer. The brief respite from thinking is interrupted by the Second Messenger who pushes into the crowd and tries in breathless monosyllables to warn the people of the despicable Conqueror "who brings his own enemy!"

> At every road corner—
> A figure of horror
> With blood for his color:
> Fist for his hand:
> Reek where he stands:
> Hate for his heart:
> Sneers for his mouth:
> Clouts for his clothes:
> Oaths if he speak:—

The Messenger's description of other towns' passive acceptance of this shame makes the crowd frantic. The people turn against the government and the leaders to accuse them of treachery. They mill about "crazy with terror."

The Announcer then describes the priests' urging the people to remember their gods, an emotional appeal that silences the angry crowd. "It's wonderful: Really impressive:" comments the dispassionate Announcer. The priest in a chant tells the crowd to give up the deluding way of reason and to turn to their gods. The people accept this plea to seek comfort in religion by going into a kind of primitive snake dance, chanting to the drums, following a young girl who leads them up the stairs to the temple where the priests are standing. The voice of an Aged General interrupts this ancient rite to urge the people to fight for their freedom:

> You are foolish old men.
>
> You ought to be flogged for your foolishness.
> Your grandfathers died to be free
> And you—you juggle with freedom!

In stirring lines he tries to make them seize their last chance to live as free men, to reject slavery beneath a strong man:

> The free will fight for their freedom.
> They're free men first. They feed
> Meager or fat but as free men.

He warns them there are "still inches for fighting." They have a choice. Either they die, or their "children will crawl for it!" The crowd refuses to listen; the square fills with deserters and stragglers; individual voices express acceptance of defeat, call the General's words, "Opinion and talk." They prefer a strong leader, believing "The age demands a made-up mind." They throw their arms away, scorn freedom, and say, "Freedom's for fools: / Force is the certainty!" They silently wait for the approach of the Conqueror.[7]

The Announcer describes the approach of the metal-clad leader, his "eyeballs hollow," and his armor also empty: "There is no one at all there: there's only the metal:" The people refuse to see. They lie on the pavement.

> The people invent their oppressors: they wish to believe in them.
> They wish to be free of their freedom: released from their
>   liberty:—

When the armored arm rises, the people shout with joy: "The city of masterless men has found a master!"

MacLeish achieves a feeling of doom from the first report of the resurrection of the dead woman, her prophecy, and the reactions of the mindless masses of people who have not the will to fight for their freedom. The Announcer, impressed by his own words, contrasts first with the urgency of the Messengers who try to alert the people to their danger and then with the Old Soldier who tries to rouse them to action. As in *Panic*, MacLeish is suggesting in *The Fall of the City* that faith in a strong leader is based on delusion. Strength is really the sum total of courageous action. The changing rhythms in the lines for the various speakers and the shifting tempo give variety to the lines. The tension built up by speakers representing acceptance and then resistance and the mounting expectation of the Conqueror, after the stirring words of the General, is somewhat dissipated by his arrival. Something is needed beyond the description and the brief reaction. It is at this point that an imaginative director would have to fill in.

The Fall of the City was produced by Columbia Broadcasting Company, April 11, 1937, and was hailed as a milestone in radio drama.[8] The play was later described as anticipating history, the Austrian *anschluss* on March 15, 1938, having given it an almost "intolerable timeliness."[9] There were questions whether much of the good poetry might not have been lost, whether there was not, perhaps, too much for a half hour's performance. The production was staged in an armory with a supporting cast of one hundred and fifty to two hundred; recorded voices repeated through loud-speakers gave the effect of a crowd of nearly ten thousand. Most critics felt that the Conqueror's approach should have been dramatized. Gilbert Seldes questioned whether the three speeches of the Messenger were the best possible use of the dramatic possibilities.[10]

VI   Air Raid (1939)

Guernica was bombed in April, 1937. This was a town chosen by the Nazis as an experiment in "blitzkrieg." In "Communists, Writers, and the Spanish War" MacLeish rebuked American liberals for refusing to see the difference between attacks in 1914 and in 1937. "In 1914 the methodical and murderous shelling of the civilian population of a Spanish sea-coast town by a German fleet would have been an act of war. In 1937 it is not an act of war. The Spaniards merely die, and the Germans sail away. In 1914 the massacre of the civil population of an undefended Basque village by German planes would have been an act of war. In 1937 it is not an act of war. The Basques merely lie kicking in the fields where the machine guns caught up with them, and the Germans fly away."[11] MacLeish saw that in this undeclared war the prestige of the fascist powers was at stake. In *Air Raid* (1939) he dramatized the detached, unfeeling, impersonal reaction of one who observed—and the implication is much wider than just the character of the impersonal Announcer—the actual "methodical and murderous shelling" of a Spanish town.

The Studio Director alerts the radio listeners to the target, "one of those old-time hill-towns" where the big show is about to take place. Commenting upon the turn civilization has made, he sets the tone of irony which pervades the play:

They called their warfare in the old days wars
And fought with men and men who fought were killed.

We call it peace and kill the women and the children.

The Announcer from his safe vantage point objectively describes the setting, a town twenty-eight miles from the border, flooded with brilliant sunshine, whose men have gone to the fields and whose women fill the square with their chatter and laughter. He picks up snatches of conversation which describe the people and their concerns: women fussing over the wash; a boy calling "Harry! Be quick Harry! Be Quick! Quick!"; an old woman philosophizing about weather and haymaking; girls gossiping about men, love, and marriage; wives chiding their men for always talking about war. This carefree talk and laughter are intermittently interrupted by a woman's vocalizing.

The Announcer continues his dry report, guessing the number of planes and their possible speed, of a town unaware of what is about to happen:

> They are flushing the cobblestones with water.
> The sidewalks are slippery with sun.
> It smells of a summer morning anywhere:
> It smells of seven o'clock in the morning in
> Any town they water dust in.

A sick woman wanting to die recalls to a boy her girlhood memories of war, confused with domestic concerns and a few bright personal flashes. The boy keeps saying, "They kill the children when they come. I've read it."

The Announcer, excited by the technical achievement and completely unaware of the human significance, breaks in with an excited report of the camera's spotting a plane. His description is lyrical: "Spark in the sky when he hangs and the / Sun angles on the fuselage:" There is ironic contrast in the momentary and safe-seeming joys of happy young lovers. A siren in the distance parodies the woman's voice, and the Announcer casually observes that the listeners have but ten minutes to wait. He makes an estimate on the number and speed of the planes. Women's querulous voices complain about the racket, the talk of war, and the crazy officials that cannot run a government quietly. Domesticity is their whole concern. "A woman's got no time to watch the wars," they say. When a police sergeant

pompously orders the women into the vaults, they shriek at him
derisively: "And who'll be watching the pot while we're squatting
there / Counting the mother spiders?"

The contrast between the sergeant's attempts to reason with
the women and their shrieking, derisive laughter is interrupted
by the distant explosion of anti-aircraft. There is further irony
in the Announcer's clipped report of the approaching planes
which is interspersed with a woman's mocking comments about
the iron man's photograph in which his fist and his chin protrude.

Sure that the planes will pass over, the women crowd into
the streets and flutter their skirts in sign of welcome. Against
the brutal roar of the engines the Announcer impersonally describes the formation of the planes as if he were explaining a
fast play in a ball game:

> They swing: the wing dips:
> There's the signal: the dip: they'll
> Dive: they're ready to dive:
> They're steady: they're heading down:
> They're dead on the town: they're nosing:
> They're easing over: they're over:
> There they go: there they—

For a moment the shrieking voices of women mingle with the
shattering roar of machine guns; then the planes fade into a long
musical note; finally they disappear into the silence. After the
quiet settles, all that is left is a boy's voice again calling, "Harry!
Harry! Harry!"

Air Raid is an effective play. In a brief span MacLeish has
communicated the life in a small town on a summer's morning
and contrasted it with the ruthlessness of the bombing experiment. The detachment of the Announcer, his impersonal interest
in the newsmen's cameras and in the approaching planes, and
his unconcern for the plight of the women, the boy, the lovers,
or the police sergeant, illustrate the mood of a time far advanced
in technology but callous in its understanding of the significance
in human terms. The play is an ironic comment on twentieth-
century mechanical progress and the desiccation of human
feeling.

MacLeish explained how he tried to achieve a kinetic effect
in the sound of the raid: "I have tried to do what the composer
does; to have recurrent phrases, as in a symphony. For example,
the sirens and drone of the planes give the play a sound curve

or definite sound pattern. These recurring themes knit the drama and pull all sounds of the play along the line the action is moving."[12]

His enthusiasm for the possibilities of radio drama, expressed in the Foreword to *The Fall of the City,* was somewhat tempered by experience. In an interview following the production of *Air Raid,* he deplored the amount of time and effort expended for a single half-hour performance. The play represented six months of work in writing, several weeks of lengthy rehearsal, and a considerable financial investment.

MacLeish was given credit for anticipating history. The play was written in June, the invasion of Czechoslovakia occurred in September. A *Time* writer observed, "In spite of the fact that the situation is a straight projection of last month's Czechoslovakian crisis, when a man listened for war at his loud speaker like a frightened bellboy at a murderer's keyhole, prescient Poet MacLeish began it in the spring, rewrote it in August."[13]

VII   Land of the Free (1938)

MacLeish called *Land of the Free* an experiment combining pictures and verse, "a book of photographs illustrated by a poem." It is the poem, "the sound track," that becomes the ironic commentary to photographs which portray the lost opportunities of a free people. The work makes a shocking comment on exploitation and waste, on a national philosophy that places emphasis on action rather than on thought. The photographs were selected from studies made by governmental agencies during the years of the Depression on the condition of the land, the cities, and the people in poverty-stricken areas.

The recurring theme of the poem expresses a kind of tardy awareness: "We didn't know," "We didn't think," "Most of the time we never wondered," "Most of the time till now we never thought." The waste is not only in land but in human lives for the victims of an unfortunate economic pattern are left in the backwash in various areas or are forced to join the itinerants of the road, moving with the seasonal crops and jobs. The senseless destruction of resources is richly illustrated: eroded fields, forests leveled, "millions of acres of stumps," Kentucky grass land washed out, cities built by the saw mills and left to deteriorate, prairie rivers once rich with catfish, shad, and ducks—

Now that the ruins are back of us: back of the mud-banks:
Back of the dead perch on the slimy sand:

The plight of the homeless, jobless, poverty-ridden, one-third
of the nation points to a kind of irresponsibility in which Americans had indulged:

The stream-beds stinking in the August sunlight:
The pools sluggish with sewage: choked with tree trunks:

and behind also "the measureless pasture."

It becomes a question whether, with the destruction of the
land, liberty has not also gone; whether the American dream
was not closely associated with building a new life on new
land. It becomes a question whether liberty was not arrogantly
abused when coupled with irresponsibility. Certainly all that
was left for many in the depressed 1930's was "the narrow acre
of the road." Since there is no longer the West and fresh opportunity, MacLeish raised the question whether the American
dream of liberty is told only by the gravestones. The book closes
with the hope of another dream of liberty, one based not on the
land, which has been so carelessly exploited and destroyed, but
on the people.

The poem reflects MacLeish's ear for contemporary idiom
and speech, and it is an attempt to evoke the emotion and
thought of desperate people photographed, pictures which he
called "vivid American documents." The *Christian Century*
commented on MacLeish's deep concern for people and on his
"poignant and piercing lines" in these studies of the uprooted
and transient.[14] The reviewer in *Time* called the photographs
"the most excoriating testimonial" of what the United States
citizens have done to the continent.[15]

VIII America Was Promises (1939)

The term "public speech" most aptly applies to the long,
discursive poem *America Was Promises* which expresses with
somewhat greater abstraction the ideas stated in *Land of the
Free*. It is difficult to believe that this poem was written by the
poet who wrote "You, Andrew Marvell." There is a certain
similarity between the two poems: the movement from East to
West, from an older civilization to one more recent, each one
having its moment and then passing its heritage to the next.

But there the slight similarity ends. The concentration in the later poem is on the American story from the Jeffersonian dream to the disillusionment of the 1930's, with a concluding hopeful challenge to the American people.

The poem is a pastiche of sense impressions, of rhetorical questions, of abstract statements about the direction democracy has taken, several sharply designed vignettes, and a few oracular conclusions. It would be difficult to quarrel with the central idea that the great possibilities of America were destroyed when the government directed attention to protecting special interests rather than to concerning itself with the good of all the people. But the effect is scattered.

To the repeated question, America was promises to whom, the answer seems to be for those who took them. When Jefferson looked upon the virgin country, he declared

> The promises were Man's: the land was his—
> Man endowed by his Creator:
> Earnest in love: perfectible by reason:
> Just and perceiving justice: his natural nature
> Clear and sweet at the source as springs in trees are.

But "Man" did not seize the moment. There was a change when in Philadelphia "Man" dwindled into "men" who "turned promises to capital"—

> Practicing prudence on a long-term lease:
> Building liberty to fit the parlor:

Old Man Adams knew about the promises of America and how it "turned enlightened selfishness to wealth." The kind of Americans produced by the worship of money MacLeish describes as follows:

> Card sharps: well dressed women: dancefloor doublers,
> The Aristocracy of Wealth and Talents
> Sold its talents: bought the public notice:
> Drank in public: went to bed in public:
> Patronized the arts in public: pall'd with
> Public authors public beauties:

Tom Paine knew that the promises were for the People—"Whatever was truly built the People had built it"—but they did not speak. The people left the speech to the lawless or to the "coarse ambitious priest" who did not tell the truth. MacLeish

suggests that Americans not go back into history for the answers
—to Jefferson, to Adams, to Tom Paine—but that they recognize
the great promises of the moment: *"The promises are theirs who
take them."* The oratorical quality of the lines which follow
perhaps best illustrates the difference between the evocative
strength of the earlier lyric "You, Andrew Marvell" and the
broad generalities of public speech in the later poem:

> Listen! Brothers! Generation!
> Listen! You have heard these words. Believe it!
> Believe the promises are theirs who take them!

Richard Eberhart, reviewing the *Collected Poems 1917-1952*,
described the poem as the culmination of MacLeish's polemicist
period. When the poem first appeared, this critic reacted
strongly against it as a political poem; he admitted that he
liked it better on a later reading.[16] J. M. Brinnin commended
the poet for his identification with progressive elements in
politics and for being able, in exhortation like *America Was
Promises,* to keep something of his "felicity of cadence, the
peculiar and resourceful faculty for translating native beauty."[17]
America Was Promises was set to music by Nicolas Nabokoff,
who collaborated with MacLeish on the ballet, *Union Pacific.*
It was performed on the Columbia Broadcasting System "Work-
shop," April 5, 1940. The composer described the poem as
didactic, the emotional content ranging from tender lyric to
passionate anger.[18]

MacLeish reacted to the depression which impoverished one-
third of the nation, and he reacted to the alarming increase of
Nazi power in Germany. He identified himself with economic,
social, and political problems; he spoke directly about the issues.
These poems were written to reach a large public, carrying an
overtone of urgency. Their oratory and the large generalizations
roused the negative criticism of the time. MacLeish later
explained why the "political art" of the 1930's was unpopular
in artistic circles as well as political. It was not that the artist
was Communist, or "a clerical fascist," or a New Dealer; he had
proven himself "aesthetically unreliable." Having violated "the
American mystique," he was not a pure artist. He was, instead, a
political man.[19]

CHAPTER 5

Poet in Public Life

I

BETWEEN 1938 and 1949 MacLeish served in a number of capacities not usually the lot of a practicing poet. This eleven-year span brought duties that tested his ability not only to work with groups of people of widely different interests and points of view but to organize and reorganize a major public institution, and also to serve as chairman and editor for planning groups charting a completely new international organization. In this decade, when the United States was involved in World War II and was in the planning stage of the United Nations, MacLeish as an active liberal identified himself with the spirit and the problems of the time. In magazine articles, in speeches, in addresses and lectures, and in poetry, he focused his attention upon the precious experiment that was American democracy and upon the dangers inherent in the renunciation of political responsibility.

In February, 1938, he became curator of the Nieman Collection of Contemporary Journalism at Harvard University and adviser to the Nieman Fellows. The Nieman Fellowships, a memorial to Lucius Nieman, founder of the Milwaukee *Journal,* are designated for working newspaper men and women. The first fellowships were awarded during the college year of 1938-39 so that Archibald MacLeish became associated with a new and continuing, valuable educational venture.

His appointment as head of the Library of Congress, after noisy opposition, was ratified by the Senate. He served from October, 1939, until 1944. President Roosevelt appointed Mac-Leish to the directorship of the Office of Facts and Figures early in October, 1941, an appointment to run concurrently with his position as Librarian of Congress. The President wanted an organization that would coordinate reports from several government departments and present to the American people a more coherent picture of the Administration's defense and foreign policies. The director was given immense responsibility

but no executive power to suppress or clarify conflicting reports.[1]
MacLeish became an easy target not only for political rivals
but for professional reporters resentful that an untrained newspaper man was placed above them. They sometimes fought by
writing parodies of his poetry. When the Office of War Information took over the Office of Facts and Figures in 1942, MacLeish
continued to work as assistant director under Elmer Davis until
January, 1943, when he resigned to give full time to the Library
of Congress.

In June of 1942, when he was Librarian of Congress as well
as assistant director of the Office of War Information, MacLeish
gave the Rede Lecture at Cambridge University. Traditionally
the lecturers are given six months notice to prepare scholarly
papers. MacLeish was given three days. He spoke on isolationism, an issue of extreme urgency at the time. He said that
isolationism was dead but that "old isolationists never really die;
they merely dig their toes into new positions. . . . The new
position, whatever name is given it, is isolation still. Where the
old isolationism opposed the country's determination to face the
war, the new isolationism opposed the country's determination
to face the peace. Drawing the lines along that issue shows the
issue for what it is."[2]

It was also during these years that Roosevelt was trying to
present to the American people the immensity of the problems
which the country faced and to awaken it to a need for action.
He made full use of radio to reach the widest possible audience,
both by public speech and by fireside chat. During these years
questions were continually being raised about who wrote the
Roosevelt talks, and the name of Archibald MacLeish occasionally appears.[3]

He served as Assistant Secretary of State from 1944 to 1945.
During the period when his qualifications were being investi-
gated, he was found guilty of being a poet. Lame duck Senator
Bennet Champ Clark asked him to explain a sonnet which he
had written as an undergraduate. The Senator was relying on
American prejudice against poetry—one "as old as the frontier's
distrust of all book learning."[4] MacLeish answered insults of
this kind when he wrote the poem, "A Poet Speaks from the
Visitor's Gallery," and reminded the legislators that poets write
history; great men in history, if not poets themselves, had sense
enough not to offend poets, "Whose songs are marble and whose
marble sings."[5]

At the end of the war he became active in the organization of UNESCO; he served as deputy chairman of the United States delegation to the first conference in Paris, 1946. As chairman of the program coordinating committee for UNESCO, MacLeish reported to the General Conference in Paris on December 9, 1946, the program which evolved from studies of several subcommissions. The difficulty of drafting a coherent and single prospectus from the mass of proposals can be suggested by the breadth of the aim stated for the organization.[6]

II *Librarian of Congress*

MacLeish had been involved in controversy with fellow writers when he defined the role of the poet in "Invocation to the Social Muse" and with the Marxist critics when he wrote "Frescoes" and "Social Cant." But when he was named to head the Library of Congress, he learned what Americans do to fellow citizens who are poets and who become involved in political appointments.

When President Roosevelt named Archibald MacLeish to succeed Dr. Herbert Putnam as head of the Library of Congress, his announcement roused noisy protests from professional librarians as well as politicians.[7] Representative J. Parnell Thomas (R., N. J.), a member of the Un-American Activities Committee, declared "that the nomination of the poet for the post was a repetition of evidence that Communist influence had entered executive appointments lately."[8] This extreme accusation brought immediate support for the MacLeish appointment from several newspapers and journals as well as from literary and political figures.[9]

M. J. Ferguson, President of the American Library Association, presented an "open letter" to four thousand delegates at the San Francisco convention (June, 1939) addressed to President Roosevelt, Vice-President John N. Garner, and the Senate, asking denial of the confirmation because MacLeish was not a trained librarian. Not only was this letter accepted by the convention but similar resolutions came from various sections. There was a flurry of letters protesting and defending the appointment,[10] but real support in favor of MacLeish came from important quarters. M. Llewellyn Raney, Director of the University of Chicago Libraries, the Executive Board of the Staff Association of the New York Public Library, and the

Metropolitan Council of New York endorsed the appointment and urged confirmation.[11] The press supported "tough-minded, tough-muscled Poet MacLeish" whose energy and administrative ability had been so ably proven in the editorial post on *Fortune*.[12] The Senate roll-call vote confirming the appointment of MacLeish by sixty-three to eight indicated the small but noisy proportions of the controversy.[13] On October 2, 1939, MacLeish took over the duties from Dr. Putnam who later said that the protests were mostly against "the theory of him" and who praised his successor "in almost poetic terms."[14]

In the forty years in which Dr. Putnam had served, the Library of Congress had emerged as a research center and "fountainhead of national culture," with holdings in various categories running into the millions.[15] It was not so much an organization, however, as "the lengthened shadow of a man." In his report published five years later, MacLeish describes what he found: the "whole fabric depended from the Librarian as a miraculous architecture of the paper wasp hangs from a single anchor."[16] There was the librarian, the chief assistant librarian, the secretary for the library—neither the librarian nor the chief assistant librarian had his own full-time secretary—and below these two men were thirty-five different and separate administrative units of diverse activities dependent on them for immediate supervision. The fiscal operations were complicated, duplicated, and difficult to control.

MacLeish turned to the experts for study and advice. Five competent accounting officers worked from the fall of 1939 to 1942 to complete a survey of operations; they recommended complete reorganization. The enormity of the operations included problems relating to personnel—appointments, salaries,[17] promotions—to backlog of orders, to cataloguing, to the backlog of Library of Congress cards not sent out to the libraries, to neglect of custodial responsibilities. Thousands of books were missing.

During MacLeish's first two years it is reported that the Library had "undergone a nearly incredible metamorphosis," not merely in the addition of the ten-million-dollar annex, but in the operation and direction of the Library itself.[18] MacLeish had already revealed himself to be a natural executive as well as a lover of books. He wanted to make the Library of Congress "a people's library of reference" because he believed that libraries should play a vital role in a democracy. He fostered the Library of Congress Radio Program which dramatized incidents and legends in American History; these scripts by library staff members were later published as *The American Story* (1944). He also encouraged recording American folk tunes.[19] In these war years he was concerned about the destruction of European libraries and joined with the American Council of Learned Societies to purchase books or microfilm of any material not available in the United States.[20]

MacLeish secured the services of expert librarians to serve with the Librarian's Committee under the chairmanship of Dean Carleton B. Joeckel, University of Chicago Graduate Library School. On the advice of this group, MacLeish issued a series of orders to strengthen weak administrative controls: in June, 1940, setting up the Administrative and Reference Department; in September, 1940, establishing the Processing Department, the Copyright Office, and the Law Library. In 1943 the Administrative Department was liquidated and the Acquisitions Department created.

This delegation of authority, seemingly simple, involved many related and complicated changes. In his report, "The Reorganization of the Library of Congress, 1939-1944," MacLeish, serving as chairman for the work of his large staff, reported in detail the evolution of three departments—processing, acquisitions, and reference.[21] Keyes D. Metcalf, director of the Harvard Libraries, wrote that the report vindicated the appointment of MacLeish to the librarian's position, revealed the enormity of the problem he faced, and the way he "plunged boldly ahead at a pace that few if any trained librarians would have attempted."[22] F. A. Mullen, director of Catholic University of America, seconded Metcalf's tribute and noted particularly the magnitude of MacLeish's job in this administrative reorganization and in the adoption of a more adequate pay-scale.[23]

In his position as librarian during the war years, MacLeish saw libraries as active agents in the democratic process; they could supply public information and thereby provide defenses against the special pleading not only from European propaganda but from the enemy within.[24] In a time characterized by "the triumph of the lie, the mutilation of culture, and the persecution of the Word," he asserted that the keepers of books could not be neutral: "The authority of art and learning rests on knowledge of the arts and learnings. Only by affirmation ... can that inheritance be made secure."[25] He believed that the librarians alone would promote adult education and could make the typical, non-radical American book borrower recognize "the existence in the United States of the kind of situation which has produced fascism elsewhere." He believed the libraries were really teachers able to encourage a belief in the American inheritance of free, independent minds as opposed to ignorant and brutal ones.[26]

Addressing the annual convention of the American Library Association three years after this group had protested his appointment, he reminded his audience how in country after country the intellectuals and the writers were first sought out to be shot or left to rot in prison and how books were either banned or burned. He rebuked those scholars and writers who "have not perceived that the defense of the country involves an affirmation, an assertion of a fighting and affirmative belief in intellectual things, a willingness not only to resist attacks upon their world and on themselves but to conceive offenses of their own and fight them through and win them."[27] MacLeish believed it possible to win the battle of arms and to lose "the battle of belief"—"the power and authority of truth and free intelligence"—to the forces of ignorance and superstition.

III   The Irresponsibles (1940)

The Irresponsibles was published in *The Nation*, May 18, 1940. There were a number of conjectures about why at this particular date MacLeish rejected his often repeated conviction that a poet must not align himself with a cause. In view of the events, detachment would have seemed inexplicable. During the night of May 10, 1940, the Germans without warning invaded Belgium, the Netherlands, and Luxembourg. By June 22, 1940, these countries and France were under Nazi rule. On that date France signed the most humiliating armistice since the Napoleonic era.

The Irresponsibles is not so much a reversal of an esthetic definition of poetry as an extension of the position taken in "Public Speech and Private Speech in Poetry" (1938) and in "Poetry and the Public World" (1939) which was that poetry is concerned with all experience from the most personal to the most complicated political and public condition. *The Irresponsibles* is a charge against the intellectuals and the writers for a failure to act in time of crisis. MacLeish states the position of the intellectuals and the esthetes as follows: "The study of beauty, of history, of science, has occupied our whole hearts, and the misfortunes of our generation are none of our concern. They are the practical and political concern of practical and political men, but the concern of the scholar, the concern of the artist, is with other, purer, more enduring things."[28]

He charged writers with an indifference to a crisis that was being clearly developed: "Nothing is more characteristic of the intellectuals of our generation than their failure to understand what it is that is happening to their world. And nothing explains that failure so precisely as their unwillingness to see what they have seen and to know what they do truly know." Writers best know what leads free governments to enslave learning and the arts, and what makes societies replace a nation's culture with private and parochial art and science. It was a time not only of practical and political crisis but also of cultural crisis: brutality, force, and lies were the weapons used to destroy the common basis of communism, respect for the individual, respect for the nationless creation of the artist. It was a "revolution of despair" against "the rule of moral law, the rule of spiritual authority, the rule of intellectual truth." MacLeish described this "revolution of gangs" as a revolution against the world of the mind.

He raised the question why there had been so little attack against this war of corruption and lies. He found one explanation in the fact that intellectuals were divided among scholars and writers. The division destroyed the intellectual's sense of responsibility. In other times the scholar-writer had been "a man of wholesome purpose, of singleness of intention—a single intellectual champion." His writing was not "a kind of academic narcissism" but an illumination of the present by its relation to the past. He cited men like Milton, Voltaire, and Bartolomé de las Casas who felt "an obligation to defend the disciplines of thought not in their own but in the general interest." If men of this kind had been alive, "the unimaginable indecencies of propaganda" would not have flourished in Germany, Russia, Spain, and elsewhere.

He gave several reasons why the responsible scholar-writers, men like Thomas Mann, were absent from the scene in the 1940's. He believed that scientific methods applied to the humanities, "destroying loyalties and habits of mind," separated the past from the present: "Past is scholar's country; present is writer's." The dilution of intellectual life in the twentieth century in such current vulgarization of knowledge as historical novels, popularized science, and digests of philosophy encouraged confused thinking. The greatest single cause, however, was that the scholar had become indifferent to values, careless of significance: "He is a refugee from consequences, an exile from the responsibilities of moral choice." The doctoral thesis has become the symbol of the modern scholar's world, conscientious work for the sake of work, "the perfect type of irresponsibility."

The despairing note running throughout *The Irresponsibles* is that in a time of brutality the artist might destroy his world by being true to himself. The real artist "thinks without responsibility to anything but truth of feeling. He observes as artist, which is to say that he observes with honesty and truthfulness and without comment." Artists do not save the world: "They practice art. Or they put the art aside and take a rifle and go out and fight. But not *as artists*." He concluded that intellectuals may have been deceived and made helpless by the best they knew—impartial objectivity, detachment, restraint, and discipline —freed from "personal responsibility associated with personal choice."[29]

In a number of other articles and speeches MacLeish directed writers to assume a responsibility to fight fascism. Speaking to the American Association for Adult Education in New York City on May 23, 1940, he described youth as being made morally unprepared for war by the writers of his own generation who had known first or secondhand the first war. He cited such examples as Latzko, *Men at War;* Dos Passos, *Three Soldiers;* Hemingway, *Farewell to Arms;* Aldington, *Death of a Hero.* These and many like them "were not only books written against the hatefulness and cruelty and filthiness of war," but also were written against the fine phrases and the rhetorical formulas by which the war was made. These books were written by men of integrity, but they immunized the succeeding generation against the aggressor who was intent upon enslaving free men; a free people cannot fight fascism unless it believes freedom good and slavery evil.[30]

These two statements, *The Irresponsibles* and "Post-War Writers and Pre-War Readers," roused impassioned response. Edmund Wilson called MacLeish a "literary irresponsible" for attacking writers like Remarque and Latzko who, if read, might have helped prevent World War II. He deplored the "declaration of moral purposes" from the Librarian of Congress and implied that the action approached the book-burning psychosis of Hitler. MacLeish, he said, spoke as if "he had never heard of the class war . . . the fundamental conflict of the contemporary world."[31] Morton Zabel described MacLeish as a man of many voices and postures, regretted the "pitch of evangelical eloquence," and traced his "acrobatic" attitude toward the war during the 1930's.[32] Burton Rascoe, in a vituperative and personal attack, saw Hitlerite tendencies emerging in MacLeish and deplored the publicity he would get when the public began reading what he had written.[33]

In the commencement address delivered at the University of Pennsylvania, June 11, 1941, MacLeish described his own generation as believing "in a predetermined pattern of life." Describing his contemporaries as "Prophets of Doom," he thought that modern man yields both his will and his responsibilities to fate; he differs from the Greek who believed in fate but also believed that man made responsible choices. He cited the novels of the time as "victim's novels." He described this curious literary aberration as follows: the victim's enemy is not the human enemy; he is the figure crushed by forces beyond his power to resist, often unnamable forces. And so it is with the books authors write about themselves. The enemy "is something that rises out of the total life of the time like the sour smoke that hangs over a great city, or something that rustles and gibbers and mews in the contemporary psyche, or something sprawled along the whole of history, its tail and huge hind quarters buried in the dark of long-past years. The enemy is 'the System,' or 'History,' or 'Life.' "[34] MacLeish was alarmed by the effect of these books as prophecies of impotence and defeat. He saw the conflict as between those men who believe in a predestined and defeatist world and those who believe man can create the kind of world he wishes for. He believed that it was the writer's and the poet's task to create the image of the world worthy of a free people.

He cited the Berlin bonfire on March 10, 1933, when 25,000 books were destroyed, as a tribute to the power of books. He commended those American writers and publishers who were among the earliest fighters against fascism, and he reproved the booksellers and particularly the motion picture industry for its "irremediable negligence" in not working to make the American people aware of the nature of fascism.[35]

IV *Fascism or Democracy*

In the late 1930's and early 1940's MacLeish wrote and spoke vigorously to rouse Americans to the nature and the dangers of fascism. These pieces give proof to his often-repeated conviction that the duty of the poet is to focus upon and to define what is characteristic of his time; it is also the poet's duty to help create an image of what life in a democracy should be. It became a habit with many critics to deplore MacLeish's self-identification with public issues, as well as the tone with which he often expounded his thesis.

MacLeish defined fascism as the *coup d'état* of a class as hostile to ruling capitalists as it was to the Marxist proletariat, a class produced by the industrial revolution and by the capitalist money system. "Fascism is in its essence a revolt of man against himself—a revolt of stunted, half-formed, darkened men against the human world beyond their reach, and most of all against the human world of reason and intelligence and sense."[36] Most dangerous because generally ignorant and violent, and unhappy because of its limited opportunities, the fascist hangs above brute labor but "below comfort and decency and self-respect." This class is found in all countries, not just in Italy, Germany, and Spain. "It attacks in the back rooms, in the dark of the railroad trestles, in the sand-lots down by the river, in the loudspeaker on the kitchen table where the grating voice of the ambitious protest rattles the pitiful dishes with spite and hate." The Nazi image of the world is "the earth thrown backward," or a "new order of Death, and new revelation of old ignorance."[37]

The dangers of fascism were increased by the indifferent, the defeatists, and the "nervous liberals" who refused to be concerned. The "Best People," peaceful citizens of good will, preferred not to be disturbed by the issues in Spain, in Czechoslovakia, in Denmark, or in France. MacLeish stated and restated his conviction that fascism—"a negative faith in obedience, in discipline, in brutality, in death"—had to be opposed vigorously by a people with a strong conviction that democracy was worth fighting for.

On November 20, 1940, in an address delivered at Faneuil Hall in Boston, MacLeish defined "The American Cause" as a battle not in France but "in the darker and more vulnerable countries of men's hearts." The real enemies of democracy were those who defined liberty in terms of property and money, as a way of doing business, as an opportunity for gaining power and comfort for themselves. These enemies would force upon the people the choice between the new cause for which people make sacrifices in order to remain free, or the alternative, the world of goods, property, and physical comfort. MacLeish defined democracy as a way of life that is never completely established but must be continually re-creating itself. "Democracy itself has never been and is not now and never can become a way of trade, a world of goods, a heap of products," whatever these products are. Democracy is not a way of trade but a dream of freedom.[38]

One of the most ticklish problems of the time related to freedom of speech when the worst enemy was the fascist-minded at home, more dangerous than the foreign enemy. MacLeish felt that the timid liberals who would protect the state by limiting the speech of both fascists and Communists assume that freedom of speech is a privilege granted to a citizen for his own profit and satisfaction. Freedom of speech was a guarantee not for the individual's pleasure but "for the health of the state." The American doctrine also allows the state to protect itself against violations: "the existence of a constitutionally guaranteed right of freedom of expression strengthens rather than weakens the hands of the state in dealing with other practices dangerous to free institutions."[39]

Two lectures delivered in the spring of 1942 focused upon the defeatist attitude prevalent at the time. In an address at the Inaugural Dinner of Freedom House, MacLeish identified the enemy: he was not only the Nazi propagandist but the American defeatist who preferred to lose the war rather than to expend energy for victory; idle women whose dinner hours had been disturbed by the war effort; sluggish commuters who only fought for golf balls; "slippery whisperers" in newspapers and hotel lobbies who seemed to want defeat. There were also the American divisionists who feared the Russian people more than they trusted American beliefs—Americans with "ineradicable immigrant mentality." Another enemy was "the newspaper publisher to whom treason itself is not detestable if by treason he can injure those he hates." Still another was the vindictive politician who would "pay off his scores" with the blood of his countrymen.[40]

In an address delivered before the American Society of Newspaper Editors, MacLeish called upon them to police editors who would destroy the government: for instance, a powerful owner who "can publish without criticism from his colleagues a secret document of vital importance to the security of his country," a document which could only have been secured dishonestly. Since the press, rather than the government, forms public opinion, only responsible editors can police the open propagandists as well as those "who follow, consciously or unconsciously, the Axis lead." Only the press, because it is free to speak, can attack the "defeatists and divisionists who strike from that ambiguous and doubtful shadow where freedom of expression darkens into treason." Only a loyal and courageous press can expose "the skulkers," the purveyors of half truths, the venal editors who use this right for their own disloyal purposes.[41]

The partisans of freedom, MacLeish urged, must seek "words of affirmation and of faith" to re-create self-respect in man and his belief in himself. In the commencement address at Union College he described the real battle of World War II as a battle of words for the minds of men. The words of the Nazi secret police were weapons of destruction: "to destroy belief in human worth, human dignity, human capacity for action: to destroy all human hope of human and voluntary solution of the problems of our lives: to destroy all confidence in human will but the one will imposed by the ruler and perfected in the State."[42] Americans, inexperienced in "political warfare," could understand an air raid better than psychological attack: "Fraud as an instrument of conquest is something we have read of only, and the power of words to overthrow nations and enslave their people is a power in which we do not altogether or literally believe." MacLeish called for "a strategy of truth" to oppose these deceits and frauds which had confused and conquered other peoples.[43] He expressed the conviction that fascism—"a negative force in obedience, in discipline, in brutality, in death"—had to be opposed vigorously by a people with a strong conviction that democracy is worth fighting for.

V *Colloquy* (1943)

"Colloquy" is composed of fragments of idiom characteristic of the colloquial speech of various sections of the country. MacLeish catches the feeling of pride which the people of each state have in their own special area and their tendency to wonder about the strange ways of others. He suggests the different tone, for instance, between the established areas like

Maine and the frontier spirit of Nevada. The variations are partly due to differences in the life on an ocean front, the Midwestern plains, the great range of Texas, and the older settlements of the Carolinas. The lines sing out in praise of "a mixed people" representing many cultures and of many patterns of human affairs that have developed according to the opportunities of the land. The poem has been described as a "choral verse in colloquialism" that recalls the conversational line of Carl Sandburg's *The People, Yes*.

VI Actfive (1948)

Actfive represents poetry written during the years of a very active public life. In it are continued experiments in verse form ranging from prose poems to highly sophisticated, patterned verse. Some of the poems reflect the concern and disillusionment of a sensitive man who has been in the position to watch American politics in action; who has spent himself in a harsh political struggle; who is shocked by what has happened to the American dream.

The volume appeared in the same year as the *Pisan Cantos* of Ezra Pound. The title poem, "Actfive," is much shorter than Pound's work, but its castigation of contemporary society is as extensive. It is an expression of disgust and weariness over what man has failed to do with his gift of mind and heart, and it closes with a sense of wonder that flesh and bone will persist despite what the past has given and what the future might offer.

"Actfive" is written in the form of a play in three scenes, and the "action" is a movement from hopelessness over lost images to a satiric revelation of images worshiped by a juvenile society, to an insight into a chaotic world created by these silly images and to the faint ray of hope over the persistence of man to live and to love. The poem opens with an epigraph that comments upon the absence of any "noble image" in contemporary life: "*with no one to whom the duty could be owed and still to owe the duty—no one here or elsewhere: even the noble image of ourselves in which we trusted broken and destroyed.*"

In scene one, THE STAGE ALL BLOOD, the images of civilized man are gone: the King unthroned, the God deported, Man murdered; and surrounding all is an audible silence. The question is raised of who shall play the hero.

> Every circle has its center
> Where the curve is made and meant.
> Every history has one to point its moral. . . .

The poet pays tribute to the images of civilized man which had formerly inspired him to achieve deeds of greatness—to symbols which seem to have been lost or forgotten after World War II. The first image was God who in the older time "gave meaning for the wonder and the fear to find!" The second image was the King and the King's Son, "In whose rule were all things real." The third image was Man, in whose love at one time "Peace had hope and fear its intercession." It was Man that "Gave history its reason!"

The second scene, "The Masque of Mummers," answers the question of who shall play the hero. What seems to have replaced God, or the King and the King's son, or Man as images of greatness are such infantile images as can be expected of an immature people: "Heroes for the fairy stories" or "Heroes for the infant's Dream! / Bedtime comforters." The poet identifies these figures, none of which is suitable for a free and mature people. "The Science Hero" is ironically described as the one who "Twists the riddle and unlocks / All the golden answers." An image which MacLeish describes as "The Boyo of Industry" is denoted as one "that hists [*sic*] the heavy stone." "The Revolutionary Hero" is an unfeeling figure "who kills the ghost already dead." "The Great Man," resembling the father image, is another insensitive figure, one suitable only for a childish people unable to make the simplest decisions. "The Victim Hero" is a strange aberration of defeat for the most powerful nation in the world:

> Scapegoat who redeems the time
> From every duty, every burden,
> Will and purpose, act and word,
> Teaching under hurt and blow
> All man's courage is to know
> Courage not avails him: all
> His strength to fail, his will to fall—
> Honor to accept dishonor. . . .

Another hero is "The State," described as an "invisible mystery" and miracle to the weak. "The Doctor's darling the big I" is the "mirror hero" described as "Theseus of the threadbare puzzle."

The final hero is "The Crowd" which allows the frightened, the wistful, and the lonesome to lose themselves in numbers.

In the third scene, "The Shape of Flesh and Bone," a painted backdrop suggests childhood's gayety, color, and happiness. This brightness does not entirely shut out reality—the shudder of surf, the wind not lifted, *"the eaves / Dripping their icicles of blood."* In the wings lurks one who will not show his face. Lines from the first scene—"Every circle has its center..." and "Every history returns upon its moral"—are repeated and developed with the idea that every age is a reflection of its beliefs: "There what flesh and bone believe / Shapes the world that whirls them round!"

What seems to characterize our time, "this rotting age," might best be illustrated by two passages: the picture of a world distorted and one of a leader who spent his strength to do what he had to, in spite of calumny. The poet gives an image of a post-war world that has discarded all values, all humanity:

> Pain the constant lot, the daily awakening,
> Beauty deprived, quiet taken,
> Love a spasm on a bench, the truth
> A gun butt and the church a gangster's mask;
> Murder by law and falsehood in its state—

Against such a world "The blinded gunner in the beaten cause" can have little hope:

> The responsible man, death's hand upon his shoulder,
> Knowing well the liars prevail
> And calumny bring all his days to nothing;
> Knowing truth has often been betrayed
> By time that keeps it, as the crock taints water;
> Knowing nothing suffered or endured
> Will change by one word what the worst will say,
> What those who listen to the worst believe—
> The responsible man:

These lines recall Yeats's angry rebuke of his Irish compatriots and their senseless abuse of Parnell, of Synge, of patriots cornered by traitors.

There are other vignettes of suffering: the sick bride bedridden and the hostage in prison who hears footsteps and later a shot fired. The distortion and meaninglessness of our contemporary world are reflected again and again—

> The huge injustice: the intolerable wrong—
> The life unmeant: the dying unremarked:
> Multitudes mingled together in one death
> And none remembered of them all: not one:—

In spite of all ugliness and suffering, "the naked human perishable heart" persists, takes hope, knows fear, and will outface the hideous world behind it and the possibility of the ordeal being repeated:

> *And know the part they have to bear*
> *And know the void vast night above*
> *And know the night below and dare*
> *Endure and love.*

In "Geography of This Time," a prose poem, MacLeish presents the alternatives: survival for the perceptive, death for the ignorant. This poem is a plea for awareness to new and strange conditions which are not clearly indicated by words or signs, and for the courage to chart new courses which the particular historical time requires. The poet suggests that man has passed the frontiers into very dangerous country where alternatives are uncertain. He repeats several times, almost like an ominous warning, the first lines: "What is required of us is the recognition of the frontiers between the centuries. And to take heart: to cross over."

A second poem, "Definition of the Frontiers," communicates the quality of the strangeness that permeates the new country: the unfamiliar wind that has an odor; the animals whose "wildness is unfamiliar in them" and whose wandering signals are "the violation of custom and the subversion of order"; "the unnatural lovers the distortion of images the penetration of mirrors and the inarticulate meanings of the dreams." There is disenchantment in "Voyage West," a sense of futility and of waste in the people's failure of nerve. The images imply that the time is past for new discoveries, that it were better that man had never been born than to find ocean flowers: "Drifted from islands where there are no islands," or, when no land is in sight, to "Smell on the altering air the odor of rosemary." Another poem, "Journey Home," seems to be the poet's assessment of a life that has been involved in times and places not entirely in harmony with his own temperament, and of a sense of waste. Whereas the opening two stanzas suggest the young poet's search for an identity, the closing stanzas reflect the mood of an older man much harried with public life:

And where is Jesus that gentle lover?
My life is blown down: the ramblers are over it:

There are poplars growing from the broken hearth.
I have come to the door of my house: I can go no farther.

"Winter Is Another Country" presents the difficult transition into the later years and the awareness of impending age. Stated in terms of autumn and the excitement of the senses responding to rich and lush fulfillment of nature and the consciousness of the year's end, the poem communicates the painful waiting for what must come. The musical lines, the melodic and rhythmic repetitions of words and phrases—a technique that critics might liken to the poetry of St.-John Perse—are characteristic of this truncated sonnet.

A number of the poems indicate the interest and effort Mac-Leish dedicated toward perfecting a lyric form: the melodic quality of "The Cat in the Wood" in which the play of words for poetic sound effect has been ingeniously contrived; the experiment in syntax to be found in "Excavations of Troy," a poem of two stanzas in which each is a rhetorical question and in which each stanza is a pattern of verbal repetitions and continuous unpunctuated lines of varying length; the contrast between the continuous and free-moving stanzas of the three-part poem on love, "What Must"; the poet's very tidy "Poem in Prose," a series of quatrains in rhyme in praise of his wife; or the delicate poems written as if in imitation of a poetry stated in Oriental character language, "Two Trees" and "The Snow Fall."

In one of the several poems stated in images from Classical mythology, "The Rape of the Swan" represents an inverted interpretation of an old myth: "To love love and not its meaning / Hardens the heart in monstrous ways." Those who betray the meaning of love, who love only themselves or a dream of love, are often those of "hard and fanatical minds." "That Treason Crime" enlarges the usual definition to make it include an intrusion into personal privacy, an exposure to public view what decency should allow time to cover:

Those that by trick contrive
To break the house of breath,
Looting, while heart's alive,
Heart's last devise of death;

The last poem in the volume, "Brave New World," is typical of the spirit of lecture, article, and speech made during the difficult war years when MacLeish felt the time called for great men and for the large democratic vision of a Thomas Jefferson. Along with "Actfive," "The Spanish Lie," and "The Young Dead Soldiers," "Brave New World" is representative of MacLeish's political poetry. Ironic in tone, the poet contrasts the small scared men of the twentieth century with the courageous Virginian and his compatriots:

> What great men dared to choose
> Small men now dare neither win
> Nor lose.

> Freedom, when men fear freedom's use
> But love its useful name,
> Has cause and cause enough for fear
> And cause for shame.

The poem, which has the quality of public speech, is the cry of a man appalled by the indifference of his countrymen, by their failure of real commitment to the words they utter so glibly. It is the accusation of a man and poet courageous enough to be angry in poetry—facile poetry, perhaps, but intelligible and significant.

The title poem in *Actfive* and several others, although polemical in overtone, make a strong statement of MacLeish's belief that a country reflects the image it worships. He was deeply concerned about the complexity of the problems during these revolutionary years. He was also concerned about the failure of the American people to face the world in which they lived: about their failure to keep themselves informed about conditions intolerable to a free people and to make the adult choices the times required. These poems are, by nature, public speech and lack the precision of the personal lyrics in the same volume. Seldon Rodman thought "The Spanish Lie" was full of the mannerisms so cruelly parodied by Edmund Wilson in "Omelet" and as repetitious as "America Was Promises." He said the poem, "Brave New World," described the world after the war which the "irresponsibles" tried to delay.[44] Peter Viereck, reviewing *Actfive*, remarked that Archibald MacLeish had helped to educate America in two ways: esthetically, by his prewar poetry; and, morally, "by his wartime role in the government as an urgently needed consciousness."[45]

CHAPTER *6*

Later Poetry and Drama

DURING THE YEARS when MacLeish was teaching at
Harvard, he wrote plays in verse; he wrote poetry; he
wrote about poetry and about teaching poetry and writing, and
he wrote about the possibilities of a democracy if Americans
were willing to assume the responsibilities of free choice. In
the early 1950's he related the American people's fear of communism to the evil that resulted from that fear. His awareness
of this terrible sickness in American political life was expressed
in verse, in drama, and in prose. During this period he brought
poetry to the public forum, and at the same time he wrote
subtle personal lyrics.

I The Trojan Horse (1952)

Any informed American in the early 1950's, hearing *The
Trojan Horse*, would have been able to associate the self-
destruction of ancient Troy with the demoralized state of the
United States at the time. MacLeish was one of the concerned
Americans who tried to warn the people about what was
happening. In "The Revulsion of Decency" (1950), for instance,
he described how a minor politician could assert for political
reasons that 205 Communists were in the State Department
and then retract his accusations until he could not even prove
one "master spy." In these years certain columnists "made a
profitable business of the sale of hate and calumny." American
courage and confidence had dwindled to such a point that
"a campaign of innuendo and suspicion and distrust" could
thrive. It was a time when "cynically unsubstantial rumors, and
hearsay suspicions" could paralyze national life.[1] *The Trojan
Horse* relates to a country in such a state of mind.

It is a play within a play. Blind Man and Girl with a child's voice stand between actors and audience, and their dialogue serves as choral commentary on the action. The play opens with the Girl's query:

> Old Poet, old blind wandering man,
> Tell me why that town is fallen:
> Tell me by what force it fell.
> I hear the gulls scream by the water.

Against the gulls' screaming at the dead, the Blind Man explains that the city fell because the wooden horse was brought into the city and because the Swan's daughter "knew and would not know." The crowd represented by types—Child, Woman, Man, Young Woman, Girl, Boy—comment on the monstrous thing outside the city walls. Most of the women believe the horse is the work of God. Two men representing two points of view argue about the reasons for which men risk their lives in war. On the legend of Helen and Paris, one says

> So we fought for their right to be happy!
> Curious thing to be killed for:
> The right to choose and be happy!

It is this self-reliant one who asserts, "We help ourselves in this city." After ten years of war and heavy casualties they and the town still stand. The other man says men risk their lives for

> Peace! Order! Certainty!
> Things in their proper places!
> Respect for authority! Truth!
> A war like that can be won,—

He believes a god would help men fighting for those reasons, and he urges the horse to be brought in.

The people wait for the Councillors—"Each with his mind made up," the Blind Man ironically observes—and argue about whether or not Cassandra is mad. The First Councillor, the king's man, asks of the others what must be done. The Second, thinking the Greeks fled because they feared this monstrosity, urges that it be received: "What the Greeks fear must be friend to Troy." The Third Councillor argues that if the horse "Is His or comes from Him and we befriend it / God will befriend *us.*"

Laocoön, the man who can stand alone, believes God is represented by the spirit within each man and not by a monument:

> I thought Troy's horse was carved upon a coin,
> An image on a ring, that each man fingered
> Privately and as his heart was moved.
> No Trojan would have made Troy's horse a monument,
> Enormous as a public tomb. . . .

He concludes by saying, "Troy was not worshipped: Troy was
loved. . . ." The Third Councillor, impressed by these words,
changes his mind and agrees with the dissenter. When Laocoön
is asked for judgment about the horse, he says fearlessly, "Let it
be toppled / Headlong from that cliff into the sea, / The horse
and all it holds."

When the people angrily accuse him of treason and blas-
phemy, old Laocoön boldly answers: "There is a hidden word
that you must hear / If Troy is not to perish. Not my word!—"
He then hurls his spear against the belly of the horse. The
people hear a man's cry stifled, then silence. Laocoön in the
meantime has left. The Blind Man ironically comments: "His
work is done. They know the truth now. / They know what god
is in that monument."

The people mill around the great thing, "Angrier with themselves than it!" The Girl asks the Blind Man what Cassandra
muttered when she heard the stifled voice inside the horse. He
repeats the enigmatic lines of the prophetess. When the report
is brought that the sea serpents have destroyed both Laocoön
and his sons, the Councillors, whose minds were made up before
the beginning, are quick to interpret their destruction as judgment against their peer for questioning the great horse. The
Blind Man ejaculates bitterly, "Councillors should speak for
counsel. / Why do they menace us with words?" The Councillors
threaten and confuse the people who are no longer sure they did
hear the stifled cry. They hysterically accuse one another of
treason and finally out of fear allow the horse to be brought
closer. There is another warning. Beneath the noise of the heavy
wood, there is another sound. The people grow alarmed; they
recall a stifled cry. Again the Councillors threaten them into
action and, "deceived by their own senses," sneer when the
people call for Helen.

The Blind Man says of her, "Treason betrays itself with
women, / And most with those most beautiful." The people

ask her to call her husband's name. Helen, who claims to love Troy more than any Trojan, looks with disgust at the "monstrous, / Staring, swollen, image." She says she loved Troy because the city chose one man's happiness rather than the oracle that pronounced its doom. She says Menelaus has no reason to answer her by coming to destroy the town. Finally, urged by the King's Councillor to speak the names of Troy's enemies, she calls to Odysseus and to Menelaus. She stares in silence, stunned by what she hears; and then, without one word to the people, she runs away. The Blind Man explains her dilemma:

> If she should tell the truth these Trojans
> Mad in their terror would destroy her.
> If she is silent, then these others—
> Those that have hunted her so long—
> Will take her in the night.

The people who knew but would not understand, who rejected the warning of Laocoön and did not question Helen's strange behavior, are misled by the advice of the Councillors. The play closes with Cassandra's prophecy:

> What hand is that upon the bridle?
> What voice cries out Destroy! Destroy!
> Who rides the horse that has no rider?
> No other hand shall burn Troy!

II This Music Crept by Me Upon the Waters (1933)

The Trojan Horse focuses upon the political sickness of a people deluded by a terrible idea. *This Music Crept by Me Upon the Waters* is a play concerned with an image held by many Americans that prevents them from fully realizing their own lives.

This second play is set on one of the islands in the Antilles on the night of a full moon. The scene is the patio of a small but elegant house overlooking the sea. The hosts and one couple, waiting for other dinner guests, have been talking about man's search for contentment, his pursuit of the island paradise. The action of the play illustrates the capacities of various people for achieving happiness and their reactions to it. Chuck Stone, the host, has the kind of objective mind that enables him to plant palm trees so exactly they would frame the rise of a February moon. He is looking forward to that "some day" when his garden will be beautiful. His wife Elizabeth, a highly sensitive young woman, is at the moment somewhat hypnotized by the moonlight night. She seems to be waiting for something; she appreciates the way in which the natives can seize the present moment: "They have no time to lose. They live / Now. Not late, not soon, but now." She admires the way they are able to concentrate all their strength and sweetness into one moment: "To burn the heart out with its happiness!"

Oliver Oren, an Englishman, peevishly waits for the tardy dinner guests, for his stomach is more demanding than the moon. For him, every topic is a cue for a witticism or an allusion. The most articulate of the group, he belongs to a culture in which an exchange of ideas and good talk are a way of life. His observations on the pursuit of happiness and its consequences illuminate the central idea of the play. Alice Liam, like Oliver, about ten years older than the Stones, indulges in lyric enthusiasms over the beautiful evening. She is more verbal than responsive.

Elizabeth describes the Arawaks, the Indians whom Columbus found, as gentle creatures, "witnesses of human innocence: / The primitive happiness of mankind." Oliver shrewdly observes that, after the white man took the island, the Negroes worked "half-naked in the cane," and the Americans lay "stark naked on the beaches." He comments on the American preoccupation with the right to happiness and on the continuing pursuit of something brighter somewhere else. Paradise, where "Everything that will be, is," is a condition to be sought rather than to be found:

> In Paradise
> Everything is here, is this:
> The ordinary heart can't bear it.
> Suffering, yes: suffering we endure.
> But happiness! Happiness is long ago
> Or far away or not yet come to.

He believes that happiness demands "a far more rigorous discipline / Than any the meek church acknowledges." As proof of what the pursuit of happiness does to people, he describes both English and Americans at the resorts:

> The wreckage of the right to happiness
> In painted shirts and canvas trousers
> Drinking Pernod before breakfast,
> The possibility of Paradise so terrifies them!

When Chuck defends drinking as a way of passing the time, Oliver replies:

> Happiness is difficult.
> It takes a kind of courage most men
> Never are masters of, a kind of
> Innocent ruthlessness that lives
> Like leaves in the instant of the air:

Elizabeth's emotional response to the rising moon seems, among the group present, the most desperate search for intense experience. Her mood is broken by the arrival of two couples, Colonel Harry Keogh and his wife Sally, and J. B. Halsey and his wife Helen, who are more or less conventional and objective Americans who seem to need rum, social life, or a beautiful night to fill in the time. They are not the "saints of a far more rigorous discipline" who could endure an intense interval of happiness. Chuck takes these guests into the house, along with Oliver and Alice, for more drinks, "coals of ice" as he calls them. There is a very brief scene between Chuck Stone and Helen Halsey for whom the night offers a disturbing insight:

> There wasn't any sound at all—
> No sound at all and yet I heard
> Ravishing laughter on the sea
> Like negresses: in love they say
> They shriek with laughter . . . it was horrible!

The last two guests, Peter and Ann Bolt, have not yet arrived. The impression is given through her description of them that Elizabeth and Peter have never completely broken emotional ties though both have married others. She says of Peter, "It's never now or here with Peter. / It's always somewhere else and afterward": Elizabeth admits that he is deeply in love with his wife, Ann, who is competent, beautiful, but incapable of deep feeling. There is an overtone, not entirely charitable, in her description of the marriage: that Peter's seeming anxiety for his wife may be a "proof of love's disaster."

When Peter and Ann Bolt finally arrive, with apologies to Elizabeth, Peter explains that he was hoping for something that would enable him to live on this island. Ann says: "You couldn't bear it. Not the island. / Not a night like this. I know you." Peter explains that he discovered the meaning of Paradise:

I said that what I suddenly understood
There in the moonlight, on the beach, was—
This is what it *is!* Just this!
Not something afterward or elsewhere.
You live it or you don't, but what you
Live or don't live is just this:
This, this moment now, this moon now....

He explains that all his life has been a waiting for what comes tomorrow—journeys, promises, morning, books—always tomorrow. He expresses the meaning of his discovery in another way:

We cling so to the skirts of suffering
Like children to their mothers—hold
The hand that hurts our hand for fear
We'll lose ourselves unless it hurts us!—
Making a virtue of our cowardice:
Pretending that a sense of sin and shame
Is holier than the happiness we fumble.

Ann, the sensible one who seems to understand what has happened to her husband, asks him what it is that he must do. When he seems unsure, she leaves him to give him time to think. Elizabeth, who has overheard this conversation, finds that she and Peter, apart, have achieved each on his own, a communion, have found "that inexplicable happiness / Take form and meaning and grow capable." Peter and Elizabeth exchange vows to continue this "blinding instant" which they have so tardily discovered, the two of them "Removed by some enchantment not of change / To this ... this instant ... this forever."

The mood of present awareness achieved by Elizabeth and Peter is suddenly broken by the announcement of dinner—to Oliver a very different kind of miracle—and by the discovery that Ann has disappeared. In the rather hysterical and somewhat drunken reaction to the evening, the guests conclude that Ann has flung herself over the cliff into the sea. Peter abruptly leaves Elizabeth to look for his wife whom he finds in the kitchen helping out in a minor emergency. This discovery of Ann's common-sense reaction to an island paradise is followed by Elizabeth's clear, sudden peal of laughter which "turns into an hysterical sobbing sound." Peter returns to watch the moon; Helen Halsey asserts that nothing has happened; and the guests go into dinner—much to the relief of Oliver Oren.

This Music Crept by Me Upon the Waters might be called a dramatization of the idea that concerned Shakespeare in *The Tempest* or Keats in "Ode on a Grecian Urn" or "Ode on Melancholy": happiness is a human condition which must be necessarily brief when it is intense, or it cannot be endured.

III Collected Poems 1917-1952

Collected Poems 1917-1952, which won for MacLeish his second Pulitzer Prize, is an inclusive and representative anthology. The volume covers the range of his poetic achievement from the trial flights of his undergraduate years to the varied modes of expression—lyric, dramatic, polemic—of his later years. It also includes a modest number of later, unpublished poems.

IV New Poems 1951-1952

In *New Poems* a group of lyrics about the world of nature comment on the human condition. The play of imagery in "Thunderhead" correlates the flash of lightning with the moment of awareness which can involve the whole man, heart and mind. The elusive quatrains of "The Triumph of the Shell" (the poem has a subtitle: "on a picture by Ellen Barry") play upon images of worm-shell, soul-skull and suggest the immortality of song:

> Someone has gathered a shell,
> A blue veil, broken
> Fragments of shell, sand.
> Someone has spoken
>
> saying
> The skull of the shell is crowned
> With the blue veil of my love
> Because of the sea that resounds
> In the winding ear of the shell;
>
> saying
> The worm is wound in the shell
> As the soul in the whorls of time:
> Time in its spiral turns,
> The worm delights and dies;
>
> saying
> The worm with his pushing pride
> Went in at the gate of the shell:
> That season when he died
> Eternity befell;

saying
The skull of the shell is crowned
With the blue veil of my love
Because of my love that resounds
In the winding ear of the skull.

Overtones of seasonal contrast appear in "Where the Hayfields Were," a poem about an old man and his little daughter who are burning the meadows:

Coming down the mountain in the twilight—
April it was and quiet in the air—
I saw an old man and his little daughter
Burning the meadows where the hayfields were.

Forksful of flame he scattered in the meadows.
Sparkles of fire in the quiet air
Burned in their circles and the silver flowers
Danced like candles where the hayfields were,—

Danced as she did in enchanted circles,
Curtseyed and danced along the quiet air:
Slightly she danced in the stillness, in the twilight,
Dancing in the meadows where the hayfields were.

"The Rock in the Sea," a far more serious poem, recalls the image of an indifferent universe in the early sonnet, "The End of the World." It is written as if the poet by tardy insight had caught the significance of the sea bird's cry in the water cave:

Think of our blindness where the water burned!
Are we so certain that those wings, returned
And turning, we had half discerned
Before our dazzled eyes had surely seen
The bird aloft there, did not mean?—
Our hearts so seized upon the sign!

Think how we sailed up-wind, the brine
Tasting of daphne, the enormous wave
Thundering in the water cave—
Thunder in stone. And how we breached the skiff
And climbed the coral of that iron cliff
And found what only in our hearts we'd heard—
The silver screaming of that one, white bird:
The fabulous wings, the crimson beak
That opened, red as blood, to shriek
And clamor in that world of stone,
No voice to answer but its own.

What certainty, hidden in our hearts before,
Found in the bird its metaphor?

A few poems catch the spirit of the times. The two-beat lines in "Music and Drum" almost capture the drumbeat rhythm and suggest in drum and music imagery the difference between primitive and civilized man. "What the Old Women Say" communicates a kind of fear that increases the grey outlook of their age. This poem treats such a timid state of mind with half-jesting raillery:

> Out there in the fighting
> Each day is doubt,
> Each night is dread,
> Dawn is disaster.
>
> Even at home in the house
> If the lock creeps in the socket
> The roots of our sleep wake.
> We lie listening.
>
> Like flood in a field it comes—
> No sound but suddenly
> One more stone has vanished,
> A dyke drowned.
>
> Never again in our lifetime,
> Never will fear end
> Or the old ease return to us:
> Childhood remembered.
>
> Never again will we wait
> Content in the dark till our daughters
> Off in the evening somewhere,
> Laughing, come home.

The poet answers in "The Two Priests," representatives of both East and West, both of whom concentrate upon death:

> *Man in the West*
> *Man in the East*
> Man lives best
> Who loves life least,
> Says the Priest in the West.
>
> *Man in the flesh*
> *Man in the ghost*
> Man lives best
> Who fears death most,
> Says the Priest in the East.

Man in the West
Man in the East
Man in the flesh
Man in the ghost
Man lives best
Who loves life most,
Who fears death least,
Says Man to the Priest
In the East, in the West.

The poet questions the abstraction in the image of the common man in "Common Man (the century of)"; it is a generalization without meaning:

Artificial voyager,
Nameless noun to give and take
Love of man for man that man—
You and me and him and her—
Neither give nor take nor can
Weep though we may and our hearts break!
Nameless, faceless hero who
Loves for us in humankind
What we cannot find to love,
Whom we love and cannot find!
What would this abstraction do
If I were I and you were you,
If one were each and each were one
And men had faces in the sun?

Two poems reflect the spirit of 1951-52. "The Sheep in the Ruins," written for Learned and Augustus Hand, is addressed to a larger audience. The straightforward declarative statements, the less involved imagery and patterned lines recall the more loosely constructed poems in *Public Speech*. This "political" poem contrasts those who live in fear and submissiveness with those who have the courage to use man's gift of mind. The submissive "flocks of sheep" live in bombed-out ruins, driven by their masters, dogs "with brutal teeth." The poet speaks directly to "You, my friends, and you strangers, all of you," and asks whether "you" will sit "like mourners on a dunghill." The poet exhorts his listeners to remember that "The work of man, the work of splendor" has not come to an end. Even among the beaten, the sheep, "One man's finger in the dust shall trace the circle." The strong image of one man alone is communicated in the last lines:

> One man in the sun alone
> Walks between the silence and the stone:
> The city rises from his flesh, his bone.

The sickness of the early 1950's is again suggested in "The Black Day," written to the memory of Lawrence Duggan, a strong and liberal civil servant of the 1940's. The poet speaks out sharply over the shameful fear that keeps honest men silent:

> God help that country where informers thrive!
> Where slander flourishes and lies contrive
> To kill by whispers! Where men lie to live!

MacLeish found in a statement of July 21, 1949, by Francis Cardinal Spellman to Eleanor Roosevelt the too frequent tendency toward authoritarianism in America: "I shall not again publicly acknowledge you." In two quatrains entitled, "Acknowledgement," with four repetitions of "Prince," he sharply and ironically addresses the Cardinal: "Prince, consider if you can / This land acknowledges no princes!"

A number of poems in this volume of 1952 relate to poetry, to literary figures, to the state of literature in our time. Poetry in "Words in Time" is defined as a moment caught between sleep and waking: "The poet with a beat of words / Flings into time for time to keep." The different perspective in time felt by the young and the old poet is caught in the poem, "They Come No More, Those Words, Those Finches." In a poem written to the memory of André Gide, "What Riddle Asked the Sphinx," the writer's search for deeper meanings perplexes the Sphinx, "Stone deaf and blind," as if to make her wonder if the "hermit," the "traveller," has "divined / Some question" she had not set. She asks her perennial question, for which she has the answer, "What riddle is it has for answer, Man?"

There is a quality of healthy laughter in poems like "Ezry" and "The Renovated Temple." "Ezry" catches in four quatrains not only the shocking arrogance and folly of Ezra Pound and his achievement but also the difference in stature between him and "the more cautious critics" who thought well of themselves when from high places they spat upon the fools below. Pound, on the other hand, "found the mark / That measures altitude above / Sea-level for a poet's work." The poet praises this man: "You gauged the steep declivity, / Giddy with grandeur where you stood."

"The Renovated Temple"—a public speech directed to a large audience—conveys the difference between the live, lusty quality of Greek poetry and the egocentric type of modern poetry in which "the temple" has become "a private club" inhabited by "Only those pimply boys who breathe / Sour as cooky dough." They do not look out; they look within: "mirrors where the windows were."

> It's a neat place, Ma'am. They've stuffed the hawk
> And hung the oars up varnished and they talk:
> God, how they talk!—about the members and their stations,
> About the house rules and the regulations,
> About their battles with the mice and spiders—
> They talk of anything but what's outside.
> The coal-fire tinkles and the tea-cup lulls.

And still the boys wonder why the goddess never comes.

There is the enigmatic laugh of Li Po in "Poet's Laughter," and the amused laughter at the artist, or the critic, who is trying to identify a "masterpiece" in "The Snowflake Which is Now and Hence Forever":

> Birdseye scholar of the frozen fish,
> What would he make of the sole, clean, clear
> Leap of the salmon that has disappeared?

A more serious bit of humor in "The Dichter as Doktor" identifies the current sickness as introspection, a kind of mirror staring—a faulty image made by one kind of poet.

"Hypocrite Auteur" has been called a reply to T. S. Eliot that makes the replies of younger poets sound like "childish tantrums." MacLeish begins the poem by noting the preoccupation with death, not for the love of death, but "for the opulent pause" before it comes:

> Victim, rebel, convert, stoic—
> Every role but the heroic—
> We turn our tragic faces to the stalls
> To wince our moment till the curtain falls.

MacLeish then states in poetic form what he has elsewhere said about *The Waste Land*: an age perishes when the image no longer has meaning—"A world ends when its metaphor has died." He then illustrates his point by recalling images from the past that no longer speak to our time: Botticelli's image of the child and manger; Sophocles' king and "God's purpose in the terrible fatality of chance"; the myth of the girl and the swan. These metaphors have sound but no meaning; nevertheless we, "like parasite crabs," put faith in these discarded shells. By questioning whether the age "that dies upon its metaphor" is ours, he suggests that the new "presence" will be within man himself:

> Earth turns us still toward the rising east,
> The metaphor still struggles in the stone,
> The allegory of the flesh and bone
> Still stares into the summer grass
> That is its glass,
> The ignorant blood
> Still knocks at silence to be understood.
>
> Poets, deserted by the world before,
> Turn round into the actual air:
> Invent the age! Invent the metaphor!

These new poems of 1951-52 represent the range of Mac-Leish's poetic achievement and give proof that his involvement in political affairs did not damage his lyric gift. These later poems indicate a sensitivity to personal relationships and to public questions as well as a capacity for healthy laughter at follies and pretentions.

Charles Poore wrote that Archibald MacLeish is "the Renaissance Man of the Lost Generation" who throughout many careers "has remained in the tradition of the Renaissance, a man who writes memorable verse while old worlds are dying and new worlds are being born. In range and grasp of technique and ideas he is the most significant American poet."[2]

Richard Eberhart said, "The best of Archibald MacLeish's work takes poetry out of the library and, while it does not hand it to the man in the street, it offers a highly intelligible style to the many rather than the few, and is best when it is non-political." As for MacLeish's style, Eberhart wrote: "There is a plain line, from which one seizes the meaning as it flies. The pleasure is direct, simple, and may be forceful." This line, of which there are hundreds of examples, "deals with what it touches resiliently and intelligently, always sensitively. It states more than it evokes." Another kind of line which appears less frequently is "the line of the deep evocation, the rock-spring. To these mysterious lines, these strange pervasive images, one returns again and again. They have always new meanings, subtle shifts of significance as the years change the body and the mind." MacLeish "is not a mysterious poet, not seminal in that sense. He lacks some quality of suffering, and must pay for an objective ability with some lack of subjective depth."[3]

I. L. Solomon highly praised the musical qualities of the verse, the masculinity of the lines, the magnificent blank verse rhythms, the technical excellence of many verse forms from the terza rima adaptations to the simplest iambics. He credited this accomplishment to years of apprenticeship and experimentation. He described MacLeish as not only a master craftsman but also a man of ideas and of feeling, a man with "an incisive knowledge of man living in his time and before him." Mr. Solomon, as did most of the critics, believed that the personal lyrics were the best poems.[4]

Hayden Carruth remarked about the way critics "with unembarrassed abandon" had "hacked away" at MacLeish's public poems. He granted that they were much better than many of the poems written during the depression years by poets "inspired by liberal enthusiasm." He described poems like *America Was Promises* and "Colloquy for the States" as "almost propaganda" and as having "a forced folkishness and a loss of control." And yet, Carruth called reading the last anthology "a humbling experience.... Perhaps there wasn't anything wrong with him in the first place."[5]

Kimon Friar, writing about the "Protean nature of MacLeish," said: "He is much to be praised for his passionate determination to live as a whole being, and for his willingness to bear failures as well as the successes which any determined mode of action entails, to accept the possibility of crudity and sentimentalization of judgment as well as the successes of noble leadership." He described MacLeish the poet as primarily "a man of passion and compassion, a craftsman of integrity."[6]

V   Songs for Eve (1954)

This slender volume of lyrics, *Songs for Eve*, makes an optimistic statement about man's possibility as a human being, at a time when cynicism is the current fashion. In a series of twenty-eight poems MacLeish defines what life and man might be

and suggests the forces which hold him back. MacLeish returns
to the Eden myth he used in *Nobodaddy* (1925) and raises
questions about orthodox interpretations. Eve is not the sinner,
the cause of man's fall from grace, but the questioning spirit
that roused him from his somnolent animal state. The serpent
is the cynic which reiterates all the old superstitions which chain
man to his fears, his confusions, and his obsessions with guilt.
The serpent seems to reflect the orthodox beliefs of institutional
Christianity. The apple is not the temptation to disobedience and
sin but the medium by which man emerged out of his natural
state. Eve's eating the apple was not a disobedience of God's
law, but a rejection of a law that forbade man's awakening to
himself: Eve's disobedience was good because she broke the
"lion's law" and gave to man an intimation of eternity.

A loosely dramatic arrangement prevails in the sequence of
the twenty-eight songs. There is a series of contrasting statements, of arguments and answers, old myths and shibboleths
questioned and rejected, and a final strong statement about
the possibilities of man when he accepts the idea of the
potentialities of his mind.

The poem sequence opens and closes with the image of two
trees, the green-wood tree present to sight and hearing, and
beyond, the dry silent tree. The first poem, "What Eve Sang,"
conveys Eve's feeling of ecstasy on the night she distinguished
the limitations of time and space from the sense of the infinite:

> But Oh! I heard the whole of time
> And all of space give ringing rhyme
> And ring and ring and chime and chime
> When I reached out to touch and climb
> In spite of space, in spite of time.[7]

Life, says Eve, is the journey between these two trees, one
"olive and green," belonging to this world: the other

> Blossomed and blown
> Though wood be dead,
> Is mine, my own.

Her insight into the price of awareness appears in the cry of
the last line: "O my son! O my son!" The contrast in imagery
between "Sleep's green tree" and the "Tree that Eden never
knew"—between animal existence and man's emerging awareness—is made continually throughout the sequence.

Man can choose peaceful somnolence or a state of tense aware-ness. Adam marks the beginning of his life not when he was "moulded man" but on that day when he knew himself. The green tree warns that "Wakening is forbidden," that "Wakers will no longer rest." Eve said that before waking she and Adam "lived in time as fishes live," or "lived in space as hawk in air," like beings with "eyes of glass" that mirror but "may not see." Exile from Eden is having "eyes that see"; it is self-knowledge and also pain:

> But for your sin no tongue
> Had tasted, salt as blood,
> The certainty among
> These grapes of God.

Eve urges man to "give God thanks / For Eden sins" because the fall is not from paradise to the world but "From earth to God." She confidently describes the experience: "From Adam, browsing animal, / Into the soaring of the soul!" Out of Eve's disobedience emerged a mind that could perceive, could sense an inkling of love "not understood / But infinite." Eve not only rejects the myth of the fall of man but also Classical myths which explain the existence of man's soul—Zeus as swan, as bull, as shower of gold who fathered the specially gifted such as Helen of Troy or Hercules.

Adam voices the old superstition of souls fluttering in search of a body: "They enter flesh when flesh believes." Eve disparages the idea that body and soul are separate and insists that "wonder, bone and flesh are One." After a series of four riddles—Adam's, the serpent's, Eve's, the babe's—which question the source of man's consciousness, Eve "rebukes" her child: "Who told you that lie / About body and soul?" They are one, she insists, the one able to emerge from the other:

> You came by the soul
> As you came by the skin
> Where the raging strikes in
> And the wrestlers must roll.

It is the serpent's cynicism which rouses in man his doubt of himself, his fears of the "glimmering sky," the "vast overhead," that makes him quibble over Eve's assertion that "In body was the soul begun."

The Lion adds to the argument about body and soul the question of their relative strength. Counter to the usual legend of the flesh, "So fell its lust, so foul its hunger," he asserts that "Flesh is not the fierce pursuer." Eve tells her children—observing that all nature sleeps and that they themselves cannot sleep—that, with their conception, "*Sleep's green tree was cut, was cut.*" The serpent, paraphrasing the cynic's version of the Joseph-Mary-Holy Ghost myth, implies the meaning of man's birth and his hopelessness: Adam, a cuckold, and Eve's children, sired "by the apple," are destined to sleep "not well—not for good." It is the serpent who gives voice to the orthodox view that man was born in sin and must spend his life obsessed by feelings of guilt.

The sequence closes with six poems glorifying the potentialities of man. Eve rebukes the serpent for teaching the child "that snivelling guilt." She justifies disobeying "the lion's law" because by doing so she broke the hold of nature and of somnolence: "How else can heavenly thunder shake / The heart but if the heart awake?" She exchanged nature's time which moves from sweet, salt, tame, and bitter for another kind of time: "Eternity shall be his thirst." She prophesies that "*the apple tree will fall away*" and that her sons "will shape and hew / Tree that Eden never knew."

> Eden's tree will wither up,
> And char and in its ashes drift,
> But not one leaf will wilt or drop
> From that dry tree my children lift
> To hear the heart's rebellious hope.

These lines reiterate the theme that the Eden legend represents not a fall from grace but a liberation—an emergence from the animal of time, space, and change to man and self-knowledge and an awareness of infinity. The sequence closes with a ringing statement of man's capacity for immortality in human terms:

> Like any creature, man
> Lives by luck and vanishes:
> The chance wind takes the candle.
>
> *No creature leaves behind*
> *Husk or shell or rind*
> *Obdurate as the mind.*

Life is luck, death random.

Tell me, what is man
That immortal order can?

These closing lines reflect the Classical Greek view of the greatness of man if he takes courage in the possibility of his own mind. It is a rejection of the neo-orthodox preoccupation with man as a sinful creature, man weakened by fears, superstitions, and obsessions of guilt.

In the twenty-one poems that follow the sequence there are different variations on the theme stated in *Songs for Eve*. Some of the poems relate to poets and poetry. In "The Infinite Reason" MacLeish questions the idea of Rilke that man must "translate planet into angel," not for man's need but for the angel's. Since "Man is creature to whom meaning matters," and since he gathers eternity image by image, it is his role to "redeem the god" drowned in the natural world of time and space. In "Theory of Poetry" it is suggested that the world is to be known through the heart, not through the intellect. MacLeish in an amusing poem, "Dr. Sigmund Freud Discovers the Sea Shell," refers to "Science, that simple saint" who knows, calculates, counts—"knows the world she sees / Is all the world there is!"—and yet raises for others the troubling questions about meanings. In MacLeish's "Reply to Mr. Wordsworth" he questions whether there must be an "elsewhere" to explain "the certainty of miracles"; science has no explanation for pear blossoms on "twig's black wet," nor for "the stranger in the eyes, the soul."

In a number of poems MacLeish comments, with images derived from nature, on man's world. In "Infiltration of the Universe" he finds an analogy between the latency of the snail hidden in the liverfluke and the "immortal" wish or "the ascent toward consciousness" concealed in flesh and bone. There is a humorously ironic comment on nature's experiments in "Vicissitudes of the Creator"; about a crab the poet writes

In ring-side ritual of self-applause
The small ironic silence of his claws.

An amusing vignette of the more spectacular achievements of the modern Chaunticleer emerges in "The Genius":

> Waked by the pale pink
> Intimation to the eastward,
> Cock, the prey of every beast,
> Takes breath upon the hen-house rafter,
> Leans above the fiery brink
> And shrieks in brazen obscene burst
> On burst of uncontrollable derisive laughter:
> Cock has seen the sun! He first! He first!

By contrast "The Wood Dove at Candy Spring" asks and "lets the silence answer"; the poet asks, "Shall we learn silence in a while?"

In a very beautiful poem, "For the Anniversary of My Mother's Death," the poet draws the analogy between the continuation of a life and the eternal movement of the sea, between the impact of a mind on its community and the "Slow silver on the sand" as the wave retreats.

In contrast to the tempered optimism of most of the poems in the volume, MacLeish makes in "Ship of Fools" a very caustic observation upon man's four thousand years of history; the sordid spectacle of contemporary civilization indicates how badly it has rejected its capacity for perceiving an ideal, "the fountain of the deep," "the springs of the sea." Some of the lines almost sound like the reaction of a man nauseated by the McCarthy era:

> Gas out of guts in the muck like voices
> Blathering slanders in the house of
> State, and the obscene birds, the black
> Indecent, dribbling, obscene birds,
> Their mouths filled with excrement, shrieking,
> Fouling the figure of the prow....

"Reasons for Music," the last poem in the volume, might be said to be a culmination of a book paying tribute to man's capacity for awareness. Dedicated to Wallace Stevens, the poem is an answer to Hölderlin's query about being a poet at a time "when the meanings do not mean"—*Dürftiger Zeit*. The poet's work must be an unresting labor to impose form on "the confused, fortuitous," to impose form upon the transient that might promise immortality to men of the time. If to be a man is to be aware, to be a poet is to be a man:

The acropolis of eternity that crumbles
Time and again is mine—my task.
The heart's necessity compels me:
Man I am: poet must be.

Sara Henderson Hay praised the fresh, lucid approach that
MacLeish gave the overworked Eden myth, the strong characterization of Eve, and her "ringing defense of man's own
stature." She found subtlety, depth, charm, and a masterly
technique in the volume, qualities that have given distinction
to the poems of MacLeish.[8] Randall Jarrell thought he found
overtones of Pound, Eliot, and Apollinaire; and he wished he
could believe in an Eve such as MacLeish portrayed.[9] Richard
Eberhart found that the poems "represent innocence in maturity."
With reference to MacLeish's varied career, he wrote: "To be
able to write an innocent-seeming poetry, to possess the lyric
gift and outward flow unimpaired after a life of political action
and worldly affairs is a token that the spirit of lyric itself is
timeless, endlessly delightful, possible, eventful, worthy of
report."[10]

VI J. B. (1958)

Writing in 1955, MacLeish rejected T. S. Eliot's statement
that no play should be written in verse if prose were "dramatically adequate." He answered Eliot by saying that prose is adequate
for an illusion of the actual; but, if the dramatist is concerned
with the "illusion of the real," then he is concerned with "the
illusion which dramatic poetry can pursue." He gave as examples
"the illusion of Oedipus apart from the plot," or "the metaphor
of Prospero's island," or "Yeats' Purgatory," or *Hamlet* which
offers "a perception of the nature of the human heart." Only
poetry creates an illusion which can foster an understanding
by the mind, by the emotions, and by the senses—that is, by the
whole being.[11]

In the undergraduate verse in *Tower of Ivory* (1917) Mac-
Leish was concerned with man's interpretation of God and with
the meaning of human experience. In the early poetic drama
Nobodaddy (1925), he reflected an interest in Blake's attitudes
toward conventional religion and morality. In that early play
the serpent tempted Adam to raise questions and to use his
power of reason. This same voice, more fully developed in Cain,
made him ask what kind of God demands sacrifice of the trusting
and destroys the innocent. The sonnet "End of the World," as

well as parts of *Einstein* (1926) and *The Hamlet of A. MacLeish* (1928), also questioned the place of man in an indifferent universe. Another kind of callousness—a human kind of indifference—was reflected by the Announcer to the suffering of the village inhabitants in *Air Raid* (1939). The pattern of thought to be found in these earlier poems and plays is more fully developed in the play about the modern Job.

MacLeish compounded problems for himself when he set out to recast the Old Testament poem into a modern drama. The Book of Job is one of the most controversial in the Bible. The text itself raises innumerable problems.[12] Because of the nature of the contestants, man against God and Satan, there can be no real dramatic conflict. The extended arguments between Job and the three comforters, which consume the major part of the Bible story, are not material for drama. After the terrible sufferings of Job, his restoration at the end negates any possibility of the poem as tragedy in the usual sense of the term.

MacLeish turned to the Book of Job to raise questions about the nature of a God who would consent without cause to the destruction of a good man, the killing of all his children, and the infliction of physical suffering upon him. MacLeish seems to be raising questions whether this concept of God— the God of the Old Testament, the God of Vengeance—belongs to a world in which Germans murdered millions of Jews in gas chambers and Americans destroyed Japanese at Hiroshima and Nagasaki. "Good" Germans and "good" Americans, indifferent about their own guilt, obviously need to find another image of God, and of goodness, one that incorporates love with a sense of responsibility, one that can unite a compassion for others with a concern for the individual spirit. MacLeish, as he has asked other poets to do, seems to be casting off a metaphor that belongs to the past and to be seeking a new metaphor for our own time.[13]

As the framework for *J. B.*, MacLeish returned to the image he used in the early sonnet, "The End of the World," in which man's life is likened to a circus performance, his universe indifferent and meaningless. *J. B.* is very much like a morality play.[14] It is also a play within a play: two broken-down, ham-actors—one wearing the God mask, the other the Satan mask— observe and comment upon the lives and misfortunes of an American family. The stage is bare except for a low platform on which J. B.'s family act out their story; the stage level represents the earth upon which Satan walks to and fro, and an elevation to the right suggests heaven. During the first part of the play, a huge circus tent covers the acting area. It is like the protection of a friendly universe, or perhaps the inherited beliefs about a friendly universe. During the last part of the play, this tent disappears; its absence gives the effect of exposing J. B. completely to indifference and meaninglessness.[15] Scattered around the stage are what seem to be vestments of several times and churches. Even the God mask and the Satan mask, Mr. Zuss and Mr. Nickles, seem to be relics of the past, to be parodies of man's sometime religious experience.[16]

Mr. Zuss is an imposing, deep-voiced man of "magnificent deliberation" suitable to play a God who never laughs, who sees nothing wrong with the arrangement of the world. Nickles says that the "blank, beautiful, expressionless mask with eyes lidded like the eyes of the mask in Michelangelo's Night" belongs to God and the Creator of animals. He says God fumbled Job when He gave him a mind, made him grateful, and made him think "there should be justice somewhere." When Mr. Zuss answers that "Demanding justice of God" is rank irreverence, Nickles retorts that God's reasons are for animals, not for men.

Nickles, who plays "the opposite," traditionally called Father of Lies, but whom Zuss sneeringly describes as "the honest, disillusioned man,"[17] feels sympathy for J. B., a man given the light of reason but deprived of the answers. When Mr. Zuss indifferently observes that there is always someone playing Job, Nickles agrees; but he is appalled by the frequency:

> There must be
> Thousands! What's that got to do with it?
> Thousands—not with camels either:
> Millions and millions of mankind
> Burned, crushed, broken, mutilated,
> Slaughtered, and for what? For thinking!
> For walking round the world in the wrong
> Skin, the wrong-shaped noses, eyelids:
> Sleeping the wrong night wrong city—
> London, Dresden, Hiroshima.
> There never could have been so many
> Suffered more for less.[18]

In answer to Mr. Zuss's indifference, Nickles reiterates that Job is everywhere.

Nickles' mask is dark in contrast to Zuss's white one, and it is open-eyed: *"The eyes, though wrinkled with laughter, seem to stare and the mouth is drawn down in agonized disgust."* According to Zuss, it is the traditional image of evil, or of spitefulness, an echo from "some subterranean memory probably." Nickles answers that it is not an expression of evil, but of disgust: "Look at those lips: they've tasted something / Bitter as a broth of blood." Zuss's mask has a look of "cold complacence"; Nickles', one of pity. When Zuss rebukes Nickles for laughing, for being irreverent to God, Nickles retorts that, having seen, he cannot laugh. Having seen the world, he says, "I know what Hell is now—to *see. /* Consciousness of consciousness." Nickles repeats that it is not the little Freudian insights but the sickening rape of innocence that

Satan *sees.*

He sees the parked car by the plane tree.
He sees behind the fusty door,
Beneath the rug, those almost children
Struggling on the awkward seat—
Every impossible delighted dream
She's ever had of loveliness, of wonder,
Spilled with her garters to the filthy floor.
Absurd despair! Ridiculous agony!
What has any man to laugh at![19]

For Zuss, the Job story is a simple scene; and, unaware of Nickles' perception of the suffering involved, he directs him to play his part. These two old actors, modifications of Good and Evil, are not only rivals for supremacy but for domination over this rich American banker, the current Job.

J. B., the twentieth-century Job, is a New England millionaire who with his attractive wife Sarah and their five children—David, thirteen; Mary, twelve; Jonathon, ten; Ruth, eight; Rebecca, six—celebrate an abundant, happy Thanksgiving. The euphoric J. B. has ridden the crest of good luck; his business, his family, and his friends seem never to have created any problems. Sarah, nagged by a conscience that demands verbalized thanks and humility before God, expresses the simple, conventional faith that, if man does his part, God will not forget. J. B., intuitive like his children, glories in the grace of God. He never doubted that God was on his side. Sarah's God, who punishes and rewards, is just; but she fears her "happiness impending like a danger." The spirit of this opening scene is one of innocence, goodness, and optimism; no chastening experience has ever made this banker question the meaning of his life.

Zuss and Nickles recognize this J. B. as their pigeon, the good man to be tested to prove a point—"the victim of a spinning joke," as Nickles calls it. From their point of view, he is a lousy actor. They spar over concepts of piety among the poor and among the rich. When Zuss asserts that "God will show him what God *is* ... Infinite mind in midge of matter!" Nickles caustically asks why J. B. must suffer. "To praise!" answers Zuss. Nickles deplores man's credulity, his certainty that he "Is born into the bright delusion / Beauty and loving-kindness care for him." When he rejects the concept that suffering teaches,[20] Zuss asserts that man can best see God from the ash heap. Nickles answers that "A human / Face would shame the mouth that said that!"

They put on their masks and in "magnified and hollow voices" repeat the Biblical wager over "*A perfect and upright man, one / That fearest God and escheweth evil!*" Satan mask taunts his rival with the proposition that this good man, deprived of all his good fortune, would rise and curse him. The God mask, furious, "*his arm thrown out in a gesture of contemptuous commitment,*" gives his man over to the Satan mask: "*All that he hath is in thy power!*" Suddenly the Distant Voice prompts the faltering actor to finish his lines: "*Only / Upon himself / Put not forth thy hand!*"[21]

Messengers appropriate to each tragedy report to the parents what has happened, and both the ham-actors and the audience watch their reactions. These several tragedies are reported without emotion; the repeatedly senseless destruction of innocence makes the bargain between the God and the Satan masks increasingly horrible.[22] Sarah rebels, as she does in the Biblical story, against this ruthlessness; but J. B. does not question God's plan. The vividly described deaths of the children make the yea-saying of J. B. difficult to accept and account for some of the questions about the characterization.

In the first of these scenes two drunken, foul-mouthed soldiers, welcomed by J. B. and Sarah as David's friends, bumble words about the war's end, an unaccountable order given, the absence of "the right length of lumber." Nickles, watching the stunned parents and hearing J. B. assuring himself that it couldn't happen to him and his wife, jeers at this "pigeon's" credulity:

"Couldn't it? Suppose it did though: / What would the world be made of then?"

In the next scene the two messengers are newsmen with camera and notebook, and with them is a girl, the society editor, who protests, "I wish I was home in bed with a good / Boy or something. I don't like it." Her part is to keep the parents talking until "a flash bulb / Smacks them naked in the face— / It's horrible!" The newsman, indifferent to the suffering of the parents, only thinks of his chance for a prize story:

> How do I get the
> Look a mother's face has maybe
> Once in a lifetime: just before
> Her mouth knows, when her eyes are knowing?

The second newsman makes the report: four kids in a car— two of them J. B.'s son and daughter, Jonathon and Mary—the drunk kid was driving seventy or seventy-five. Sarah, moving like a sleepwalker, asks, "Why did He do it to them? / What had they done to Him—those children... What had *we* done?" J. B. answers that they have to take the evil with the good: "It doesn't mean there / *Is* no good!" Nickles prompts, "Doesn't it?" Sarah rejects J. B.'s certainty.

Nickles taunts Zuss about the way "a perfect and upright man" learns God's purpose for him. Zuss indifferently observes, "He can't act and you know it." Nickles, the Satan mask, which wears a look of pity, answers the God mask: "He doesn't have to act. He suffers. / It's an old role—played like a mouth-organ." Cynically, he remarks that what Job needs to see is "That bloody drum-stick striking; / See Who lets it strike the drum!"

In the scene that follows, the messengers are two policemen making their early morning report. They identify the youngest of the four children, Rebecca, as the little girl dressed in white, with red shoes and a red toy umbrella; they puzzle over the enigma of why the potter worked equally in worthies and monsters. One policeman finally blurts out the story to the parents: just past midnight they stumbled upon a big nineteen-year-old, "Hopped to the eyes and scared." They ordered him to take them to "it." Their suspicions were justified when they found the little girl's body. As J. B., holding the child's red parasol, speaks brokenly, "The Lord giveth... the Lord taketh away," the two masks argue over their "pigeon." Zuss asks why he won't act; Nickles answers that he isn't playing, "He's where we all are—in our suffering. / Only ... (*Nickles turns savagely on Mr. Zuss.*) Now he knows its Name!"

In the next catastrophe the messengers in steel helmets and brassards return with Sarah, who had been looking for her lost child, Ruth, in the bombed ruins. J. B.'s millions, the bank, the whole block are gone; only a floor remains. Still believing that he shares desperation with God, he tries to make Sarah repeat after him, his certainty, "The Lord giveth—" She rebels and shrieks, "Takes! / Kills! Kills! Kills! Kills!" J. B. answers, "Blessed be the name of the Lord."

Mr. Zuss preens over the yea-saying of J. B., but Nickles is disgusted over man's insensitivity to others' suffering; to Nickles it is indecent to be thankful when twenty thousand have been suffocated in a bombed-out town. He resents the hideous, senseless deaths of the children: "And all with God's consent!—foreknowledge!— / And he blesses God!" God, not content with this victory—according to Nickles—overreaches himself to demand "the proof of pain." When Mr. Zuss chants the equation that man's will is God's peace, Nickles retorts, "Will is rule: surrender is surrender. / You *make* your peace; you don't give in to it." Nickles seems to cling to the belief that, when man is himself trapped in pain, he will learn to "Spit the dirty world out—spit." Nickles insists that, "when his suffering is *him*," he will not praise.[23] As they put on their masks for the next test, the old Biblical words flood over them. The Distant Voice repeats the lines, concluding

> And still he holdeth fast his integrity ...
> Although thou movedst me against him
> To destroy him ...
>
> > without cause ...

The God-shadow raises its arm again "*in the formal gesture of contemptuous commitment*" and intones the words: "Behold he is in thine hand ... but ... Save his life!"

When the modern J. B. is revealed as the one pitiful survivor of an atomic blast, Nickles cackles to Zuss that, as usual, he has blundered: "Tumbled a whole city down / To blister one man's skin with agony." A few women and a girl sarcastically comment on the sufferings of the rich they have known only through news pictures and review without feeling the catastrophes. J. B., though raising questions about the blindness, the

meaninglessness of what has happened, clings to the belief that
God is just, that he himself is guilty. Sarah says that, if God
demands deception, she will not buy quiet with her children's
innocence:

> They are
> Dead and they were innocent: I will not
> Let you sacrifice their deaths
> To make injustice justice and God good!

When in her anguish she urges J. B. to "curse God and die"
and then leaves him, he insists, "We have no choice but to be
guilty. / God is unthinkable if we are innocent." When in his
agony he prays to God to show him his guilt, Nickles caustically
prompts Zuss to bring on the cold comforters "Who justify the
ways of God to / Job by making Job responsible."

The major part of the Biblical poem is the extended dialogue
with the three comforters; the modern playwright, by involving
the audience in the violent deaths of the children, increased
the difficulties of maintaining dramatic tension in the latter part
of the play. He must try to give dramatic form to philosophical
material: ideas about guilt and innocence, about suffering and
responsibility, about the relationship between man and the
forces of good and evil.[24] MacLeish adapted the three comforters into approximations of three phases of modern society:
Zophar, a fat priest; Eliphaz, a lean psychiatrist in a dirty
interne's jacket; and Bildad, a Marxist, a thick short man in a
ragged windbreaker.

They present three different opinions on the question of guilt.
To Marxist Bildad the suffering of one is not significant because
what matters is not justice for one man but justice for humanity.
History is not concerned with the guilt of one man: "Guilt is a
sociological accident: / Wrong class—wrong century—" To Eliphaz, the psychiatrist, "Guilt is a / Psychophenomenal situation—
/ An illusion, a disease, a sickness": All men are victims of their
own guilt even though they may be ignorant of it. J. B. rejects
this idea of "an irresponsible ignorance" as the cause of his suffering, for he needs to know that he "earned the need to suffer."

Zophar, the priest, says the guilt idea is necessary to man's
quality as a human being, otherwise he would vanish as do the
animals: "our souls accept / Eternities of reparation." When
J. B. wants to be shown his guilt, Zophar elaborates upon the
"deceptive secret" of guilt that may have been "conceived in

infancy." J. B. tells the priest that, until he knows the reasons for his suffering, even until death he will not violate his integrity. Zophar cynically answers that J. B.'s sin was to be born a man; to be a man is to have a will and a heart that is evil, both "Corrupted with its foul imagining." J. B. rejects the priest's answer as the most cruel of the three because it makes God "the miscreator of mankind."[25]

Still hoping for some justification for his suffering, J. B. repeats his trust in God. The Distant Voice, the Voice out of the Whirlwind, poses a series of questions to J. B. concerning the powers of God and the wonders of His creation; the Distant Voice for the second time rebukes J. B. for trying to instruct God; and the third time, again in a series of questions, the Distant Voice rebukes man for his presumptuousness: *"Wilt thou disannul my judgment? ... Wilt thou condemn / Me that thou mayest be righteous? / Hast thou an arm like God? Or canst thou / Thunder with a voice like Him?"* J. B. humbly concedes the omnipotence of God, confesses to having spoken without knowledge, abhors himself and repents.

In the original version of the play, in the scene following this "repentance," Zuss uncomfortably asks Nickles how J. B. voiced his repentance, and whether he did it for God or for himself. A scene very important in the development of the experience of Job is thus presented second-hand. At the end of this scene, in very few lines and very briefly, J. B. rejects Nickles' suggestion of self-annihilation. This affirmation of life is followed by the return of Sarah and by a brief lyrical expression of human love. In this original version there is no scene in which J. B. is made to reveal what he has learned from experience, a scene very much needed in the play and one necessary for the interpretation which MacLeish gives to the Job legend. This so-called "recognition scene" was developed during the rehearsals and was substituted for the original and weaker one.

In the Broadway version J. B., thinking over the magnificent words of God about his own right hand and its power to save him, lifts to his face the scrofulous hand. Zuss, as if he were prompting his suffering victim in order to encourage him in the belief that only in the fear of God lies true repentance and his only comfort, hears J. B. repeat the vow that he abhors himself and repents. Nickles, sickened by what he calls a forced repentance because God threw at J. B. the whole creation, rages that J. B. has forgotten what happened to his little children. In his disgust over the choice that God offered, he thinks it dubious triumph that J. B. swallowed the world rather than rejecting it. Zuss petulantly asks whether or not God is to be forgiven. Nickles with supreme insolence asks, "Isn't he?"

As Nickles turns away, Zuss reminds him of the final scene in the Bible poem no matter who plays Job. He accuses his cynical opposite of not having the stamina to finish his part in the play. Nickles replies that the restoration illustrates God's mercy to man who never asked to be born. He refuses to believe that J. B. will begin all over again, risk again "all that filth and blood and / Fury. . . ." The acting version portrays more clearly J. B.'s resolution. As he brings himself to his feet, his voice strong and firm, J. B. asks:

> Must I be
> Dumb because my mouth is mortal?—
> Blind because my eyes will one day
> Close forever? Is that my wickedness—
> That I am weak?

The two masks are stunned by what they hear, incredulous that J. B. should ask if his breathing should be forgiven. Nickles, sensing an advantage, answers, "Not this generation, Mister." Professing to be not the Father but the Friend, he tries to impress upon J. B. that death is not the worst alternative; the worst is having to relive all the senseless suffering. He reminds him of the millions who refused the second chance, who found a convenient means to end it all. None of those, says Nickles, knew what J. B. does: "Job's truth." Desperately Nickles tries to negate God's gift by saying that Job would rather take the filthiest kind of death than live his suffering life all over again.

When J. B. rejects Nickles, Zuss is triumphant. Zuss then restates the position implied by the Distant Voice that there is no resolution to the problem of "unintelligible suffering" but submission to the divine will. But J. B. also sternly rejects this pattern of submissive acceptance:

> I will not
> Duck my head again to thunder—
> That bullwhip cracking at my ears!—although
> He kills me with it. I must know.

When Mr. Zuss, astonished over what he has heard, repeats his theme that there is no peace except in obedience, J. B. defiantly answers both the Satan and the God masks: "I'll find a foothold somewhere *knowing*." He vows he will not laugh at life's filthy farce nor weep among the obedient and the meek, "protesting / Nothing, questioning nothing, asking / Nothing but to rise again and / bow!"

In the final scene Sarah, who had told her husband to "curse God and die," returns to J. B. because of her love for him. These stricken people, whose experience has shown that they are alone in an indifferent universe and that they can be sure only of their human love for each other, determine to begin their lives again. Depending not on the kind of a God who will destroy children for no reason, nor on churches where the candles have gone out, they will continue to seek the answers— to know. This conviction is stated by J. B. at the close of the play:

> The one thing certain in this hurtful world
> Is love's inevitable heartbreak.
> What's the future but the past to come
> Over and over, love and loss,
> What's loved most lost most.

In the final lines J. B. expresses the human capacity for suffering and, in spite of the inexplicable, the strength to continue to live and to love:

> And yet again and yet again
> In doubt, in dread, in ignorance, unanswered,
> Over and over, with the dark before,
> The dark behind it . . . and still live . . . still love.

MacLeish explained that he saw in the Job poem a relation to our own time, a time of "inexplicable sufferings" when millions were destroyed because of their race or because they lived in a certain city. He suggests that God delivered Job into Satan's hands "Because God had need of the suffering of Job." In the struggle between God and Satan, "God stakes his supremacy as God upon man's fortitude and love." It is man alone who can prove that man loves God; only man, by his persistence, can overcome Satan, of the kingdom of death, and love God, of the kingdom of life. Without man's love, God is only a creator. It is in man's love, says MacLeish, that God exists and triumphs;

in man's love that life is beautiful; in man's love that the world's injustice is resolved. "Our labor always, like Job's, is to learn through suffering to love—to love even that which lets us suffer."[26]

The religious implications in *J. B.* aroused considerable controversy. Charles A. Fenton commented on the original production at Yale: "The notion that the individual is superior to God—is not critically palatable to the institutionalized."[27] Tom F. Driver, after the Broadway production, described the play as suffering "from a sort of theological schizophrenia" because it began on what he thought a high religious plane and ended on a purely Humanistic one.[28] Theodore A. Webb, who disagreed with Driver, said that MacLeish began the play on a Humanistic level when he depicted broken-down "ham-actors" as gods.[29] Samuel Terrien wrote that "The Joban poet deals with the problem of faith in an evil world, while the author of *J. B.* presents modern man's reaction to the problem of evil without the category of faith in a loving God." He described Job as almost "an incarnation of an anti-God," but he also thought of him as an emasculated, piously conventional victim of fate who rarely rises above an intellectual stupor.[30] Henry P. Van Dusen took issue with both Driver and Tarrien. He considered the three comforters to be a brilliant and sound translation into the realities of our time. He did not find, as did Terrien, "an intelligent, eternal and gracious Power" in a God whose last words begin, "Who is this that darkeneth counsel by words without knowledge?"[31] Richard Hayes summarized the varied opinions expressed for and against the play and added his own reservations: "cultural piety demands each year its raw meat of sustenance."[32] Reinhold Niebuhr praised MacLeish's honest statement of the problem and his ingenuity in adapting the ancient poem to modern times. He felt that the emphasis on meaningless suffering led to the neglect of the more searching question in the Book of Job about the meaning of life and thus the "message" to contemporary man: for instance, the paradox of man's capacity to discover nuclear energy and his lack of wisdom in its use. Niebuhr pointed out that MacLeish does provide two answers to modern man: he repeats the voice out of the "Whirlwind" contrasting the greatness of God's creation and man's limitations; he also states his "courageous acceptance and affirmation of life with a modern romantic emphasis on love."[33]

J. B., published by Houghton Mifflin, March, 1958, was first produced by the Yale School of Drama on April 22, 1958; during the summer it was taken on tour to the World's Fair at Brussels and to other European capitals. The very favorable review by Brooks Atkinson of the Yale performance led to the Broadway production which opened on December 11, 1958. During the rehearsal period Mrs. Elia Kazan made one of the most perceptive comments on the play when she said that the first act had "tremendous identification" in the scenes of suffering; it had action and interaction of people that had "a forward sweep." She felt that in the second act there was too much argument, too much philosophy; the events were not dramatically developed; there was "a long presentation, statement of a point of view, followed by a comment or brief rejection." During the New York production she had reservations about the production's becoming too theatrical.[34]

Brooks Atkinson said that MacLeish had written "an epic of mankind" and he anticipated a long life for the play. He said that the playwright was not a solemn poet, and that much of the writing, particularly in the characters of God and Satan, was pungent and earthy. Some of the verse, he felt, was too compact for theater, and some of the scenes were begun in the middle. He also noted that the dignity, gravity, and simplicity of the King James Version was hard to match in modern poetry. He called *J. B.* impressive "in its valiant affirmation at the end," a play worthy of our time. MacLeish "has imposed his own sense of order on the chaos of the world."[35]

CHAPTER 7

Poet as Critic and Teacher

DURING THE YEARS between 1949 and 1962, when Mac-Leish was Boylston Professor of Rhetoric and Oratory at Harvard University, he was still oriented to the world outside the academic. He continued to write about the current political scene as it affected the practice of democracy: in the late 1940's and early 1950's it was the hysteria and fear over communism which threatened individual liberty. To this period belongs the creative work already discussed: *The Trojan Horse* (1952); *This Music Crept by Me Upon the Waters* (1953); *New Poems 1951-1952* which were added to the second anthology, *Collected Poems 1917-1952; Songs for Eve* (1954); and *J. B.* (1958). During these years MacLeish continued to write in defense of poets and poetry and to sharpen his own theory of poetry for our time. He published two major statements in *Poetry and Opinion* (1950) and in *Poetry and Experience* (1961). During these academic years he also continued to comment on topics related to poetry and the imagination.

I *The Ezra Pound Case*

In the late 1930's MacLeish spoke of Ezra Pound as "one of those rarest and purest of poets" who approached art as an artist and who confronted problems of society just as a school-master attacks the problem of stupidity. Apparently Pound thought of himself as attacking a bourgeois form in writing, but MacLeish thought his assault was more than that: "He was a wrecker to whom not merely the politely dead poetry of the generation immediately prior to his own, but the whole world which accepted that poetry, was an obsolescence, a solecism calling for the crowbar and the sledge."[1] He described Pound as a man who "was always the small-town rebel thumbing his nose at the respectability which wasn't there." Although some of Pound's later work was magnificent, "the posture interfered with the poetry." MacLeish thought that the great work of Pound was as translator and teacher and that his greatest contribution was to reprint Fenellosa's famous essay on the Chinese character.[2]

Ezra Pound received the first Bollingen Prize, February, 1949, for the *Pisan Cantos,* an honor awarded by the Fellows of the Library of Congress at the time he was under indictment for treason. The public furor over this award was aroused in good part by two articles written by Robert Hillyer who, among other statements, accused T. S. Eliot of heading a fascist plot.[3] The literary battle, more emotional than critical, settled into a fight between the old and the new critics; for there was very little examination of Pound's *Pisan Cantos.* Repeatedly MacLeish had supported the right of free speech as opposed to the domination of authority, and he granted freedom to speak to members of both the Right and the Left. He tested this theory when Ezra Pound became the center of this fierce literary battle. In the lecture, *Poetry and Opinion,* delivered at the University of Illinois in 1950, he sought to relate the *Cantos* to "an accepted theory of poetic function." His lecture takes the form of a dialogue between Mr. Bollingen and Mr. Saturday who attacks Pound and the jury.

Mr. Saturday directs his attack from three angles: literary, political, and ethical. He accuses Pound of unintelligibility, of pedantry, of obscurity; of unsavory political beliefs; of being a purveyor of evil. He accuses the jury of being highbrow, of attempting an apotheosis of the *Cantos,* a poem offensive to the majority and contrary to "the great fundamental concepts" of society. Mr. Bollingen cites as examples of poems in conflict with the "fundamental verities" some of the recent Irish literature, Baudelaire's *"Une Charogne,"* or Rimbaud's *"Les Premieres Communions."* Mr. Saturday then concedes that poetry should not be judged by patriotic, economic, political, or ethical standards. He also refuses to accept the idea that poetry teaches, yet he judges it by what it says. He is perplexed that, even though the judges found Pound's doctrine detestable, they gave the poem an award.

Mr. Bollingen says that to judge a poem "bad" because of its opinions is to make the judges censors. He states that the expectations of poetry change with the sensibilities of the age:

"A change in sensibility is a change precisely in the question which a poem asks," poetry being the one art always trying to be something more. From the beginning of civilization, thinking men have been concerned with "defenses" or "apologies" for poetry because there has been for every age a new problem for the man of his own time.

Mr. Bollingen reminds his opponent that Aristotle concluded that the function of poetry was to "raise the underlying coherence of life." In his defense of the *Pisan Cantos* he says that Pound reveals what he believes exists—"a vast disorder; a confused, bewildered, materialistic civilization running blindly and without dignity or faith upon vulgarity and death; a generation lost to its past and its future, to beauty and to grace." Mr. Bollingen observes that Pound's perception is in agreement with that of Baudelaire, of Rimbaud, of Yeats, of Mallarmé, all of whom saw in our industrial civilization "tragic disorder which made meaningless the very heart of meaning."

Mr. Bollingen deplores Pound's infantile and distorted "addiction to fascism," but he refuses to allow that aberration to discredit the insight which is in the poem. He refers to the blind spots of other great poets: the occultism of Rimbaud and of Yeats, the dogmatic opinions of Dante. It is possible for "opinions hateful to multitudes of human beings to live in a poem beside the most profound and enduring insights, where the poet's overriding loyalty is to his poet's perception of the world." Pound's "loyalty is not to dogmas of fascism but to the poet's vision of a tragic disorder which lies far deeper in our lives and our time." Mr. Bollingen supports the jury award because "the poem, with all its evil and its ignorance about it, accomplishes in some measure what a poem should accomplish."

MacLeish again came to the defense of Ezra Pound in 1956 when "In Praise of Dissent" he described the *Cantos* as "a true book, true dissent from the dead assumptions, but not dissent for its own sake—dissent for the sake of the ideal of order in men's lives."[4]

II *Communism or Democracy*

MacLeish believed historians would record that in the late 1940's an "uninformed and unintelligent" country failed to see that communism was not a revolutionary but a reactionary force, "one of several forms of authoritarian reaction ... headed back toward the disintegrating order of society and competing with another for the domination of that disappearing world." The true revolutionary force, stated by Jefferson in the eighteenth century, gave to the individual the chance to realize himself as an individual human being: "The whole movement of human life, violently accelerated over the last few centuries, has been a movement toward the separation of the individual consciousness from the common consciousness, the common sleep, the animal sleep,—a movement toward the differentiation of the individual from the community of the tribe, and, before that, from the community of the 'natural' life of universal instinct." This very fine concept of the dignity of the individual has been overshadowed by the "morbid and malignant figure of irresponsible and grasping power."[5]

Because of ignorance of the nature of communism, Americans lost themselves "as beginners, begetters, changers, challengers, accomplishers" and failed to establish a policy of their own. MacLeish repeated his thesis that the free man's choice between the two authoritarians of Right and Left is "the revolution of the individual." A whole nation would have to determine whether its objective—its image—was first and most important a free society, "a civilized population disciplined" to make a choice between authoritarianism or freedom, or whether its image was, first and foremost, prosperity and comfort.[6]

The problem of choice between these two forms—man's belief in himself or a reliance upon authority—had been clouded (in 1951) by the dogma that war was inevitable, an idea spread often by disenchanted Communists "who had left the discipline of the Communist Party but had not lost the habit of the Party's thought." The first to welcome the idea of the inevitability of war were those in the United States "whose inclination had always been authoritarian, and who found authoritarian ideas—even the ideas of their enemies—more palatable than a traditional American liberalism they never understood."[7]

Pressures against the revolutionary American idea of the free individual had been made by those who never accepted nor understood the meaning of the principle of freedom. MacLeish referred to the "deliberate tampering as characterizes the methods of at least one notorious contemporary politician," the United States Senator who was "applauded in freedom's name for assaults upon the individual freedom of American citizens." He reiterated the point that the principle of American democracy which allows the growth of each individual is still "the one wholly new and revolutionary idea that the modern world has produced, for all the triumphs in science and technique." It is an idea so new and revolutionary that half the patriotic societies who celebrate it have yet to understand its significance. American strength is in the inquiring, individual mind; and her faith is "in the infinite variety of human beings and in the God who made them various and of many minds." And these concepts are disturbing to minds leaning toward authoritarianism.[8]

In June, 1955, he described the stain of McCarthyism as "like the snail's corrosive track on a clean leaf." The most disturbing fact about that national experience was that a "sane, decent majority of Americans, outraged, yet tolerated the indecencies of McCarthyism"—tolerated his "debasement of morality, his betrayal of principles." The Senator attracted many crackpots: anti-Semites, anti-Protestants, anti-intellectuals, and those of "nervous animosity." MacLeish cited Walter Lippmann's *The Public Philosophy* as stating the real issues: whether free individual freedom and effective community were compatible. MacLeish himself looked upon the McCarthy era not as a sign of deterioration of the American dream "but [as] a small human boggling in the face of a series of startling and decisive steps toward individuality."[9]

He saw in the September, 1962, crisis at Oxford, Mississippi, (when James Meredith was denied entrance to the university) 'the denial of the idea on which America was founded—"a new liberty for a new people in a new world." He saw the Mississippians, Ross Barnett, and the state police as the real subversives undermining the basic structure of American democracy: he saw in the hatred of those faces "the passionate repudiation of the American proposition, and thus the implicit rejection of America itself." About their hatred of James Meredith he wrote, "He was a Negro, and that was enough. But to hate a man because he is a Negro is to hate an abstraction. And to hate an abstraction is to hate an idea. And to hate the particular idea the mob at Oxford hated is to deny America." Nations are made by commitments and by loyalties—and "the nobler the commitment of the mind, the higher the loyalty of the heart, the greater the nation."

He found in the Mississippi aberration not a local fault but one common to the whole nation. For fifteen or twenty years the national concern had been a hatred of communism rather than love for America. Hatred had produced organizations like the John Birch Society, the California fanatics, and the Oxford mob. The students who shouted "Communist" at the United States marshals had been brought up on anti-communism and not on the American idea, "the greatest and most powerful of all political causes, a cause which has no need to express itself in hatred for something else but only in affirmation of itself."[10]

III *The Place of Poetry in Society*

During the 1950's MacLeish was restating his thesis that the art of poetry involves the whole man, the outward as well as the inward experience. He rejected the too frequent modern conception that relegated poetry to the inward man alone and that insisted that the poet must not be enlisted in any cause, not "even the cause of human liberty." He cited the inclusiveness of the poetry of Dante, of Shakespeare, of Tu Fu; the involvement of Yeats and Swift; the critical canons of Coleridge. Faced with a tragic and terrible world, the poet must reject the art-for-art's-sake tenet and try to know and understand his own time. He saw in Yeats's rejection of the "muse's sterner laws" the rejection of the art-for-art's-sake doctrine; Yeats in a time of terrible troubles could not be a passive observer. MacLeish insisted that "the poet's labor is to bring his experience of life, his whole experience, to focus and understanding—but to *human* focus, to *human* understanding." He felt that during the early 1950's the poet could not afford to look only within himself. He raised the "question of the responsibility of artists and poets in the face of the corruption of human values, the perversion of human intelligence and the enslavement of the human mind with which the rise of the police state threatened the entire Western World."[11]

The absence of good poems and novels in the 1950's he laid to the writers' lack of understanding of the time. He deplored the point of view represented by "the avant (devant) garde [who] keep chanting from their safe position at the rear of the column"—a position from which no real poet could function. In the period since World War II when military, political, economic, and social changes had become revolutionary in scope, these writers seemed to regard the world as a "fixed structure beyond the reach of change ... a final and permanent achievement which cannot be touched or questioned." He believed that the fear of communism had imposed on a changing world a static image. This "sickness" had affected American character: "something makes man mean instead of candid, timid instead of determined, suspicious of each other instead of courageous and firm."[12]

At another time MacLeish rejected the dogma of the current American esthetic that separates art from life, and the artist from the community. "Artists are a kind of litmus paper to test the degree of materialism in any society." Art at its best is action: "there is no part of human experience, public or private, on which it cannot act or should not." The image created by a perceptive and sensitive poet could be translated into reality: "the old human dream of a possible reconciliation between the outward world of event and the inward world of conception through the act of art."[13]

MacLeish made one of his strongest statements about the need for poetry in our time in "The Poet and the Press." He said that both poetry and journalism are re-creations of chaotic fragments of experience, and each at its best is an instrument of knowledge. Poetry enables the reader not only to know but to feel. Poetry, through the power of the poet's imagination, re-creates the essential experience of the physical world so that for the "right reader," knowledge is carried alive to the heart. The divorce between knowledge and feeling is "the flaw at the heart of our civilization." Information is essential for survival in an atomic age but even more so is the feeling which information communicates. The "good Germans" knew about the gas ovens, and the "good Americans" knew the horror of Hiroshima; and yet both peoples could live tranquilly. The real defense is that "feeling of the mind" which can put itself "in the place where its thought goes, [can walk] in the body of the little Negro girl who feels the spittle dribbling on her cheek."

Great journalism can recompose and make sense of fragmentary experience. However, what poetry composes is more lasting, is larger, goes deeper, is more meaningful—but it is not contrary. MacLeish asked the reader to compare what a journalist might do about an old man and his horse with what Robert Frost did in "Stopping by Woods on a Snowy Evening." Ernie Pyle and Elmer Davis were great journalists "who would not have separated the feel of things from the look of them," and Yeats was one of the most exact observers of his time.

MacLeish deplored the growing tendency among journalists "toward an admirably dispassionate objectivity," and among contemporary poets an inclination "to detach feelings from their occasions—to pursue feelings as themselves and for their own sakes." This tendency toward the dispassionate in journalism and toward the increasing inwardness in poetry, was reflected, Mac-Leish felt, in the "numb indifference" of the public about what was happening in the world around it. Because of our technical progress, we are momentarily deluged with facts: contrast our current TV news coverage with the clipper-ship report of Napoleon's retreat from Moscow. We are becoming "less and less capable of receiving facts into our imagination." Poetry's "extravagant fancies" somehow more closely touch the truth than hard facts. Poetry, he said, has been "throwing out" new masters, but "the poem itself has lost its power in men's minds." He believed that "we have impaired the practice of the skill the art can give, the skill of feeling truly and as truly knowing." Instead, we know only by facts, by abstractions: "Slavery begins when men give up the human need to know with the whole heart."[14]

He defended the teaching of poetry because it affords "Knowledge in the truest meaning of the word knowledge." Science, the usually accepted means to knowledge, is gained through abstractions. Poetry does not abstract; it presents actual experience. Abstractions, he said, separate things and arranges them into patterns: "Abstractions have a limiting, a dehumanizing, a dehydrating effect." In a scientific society men do not concern themselves with feelings or with values: "In few civilizations have the senses been less alive than they are with us." MacLeish praised Confucius who told his disciples that the 305 songs used in the civil service examinations could be digested into one commandment—"Have no twisty thoughts."[15]

Of man's need for poetry in a scientific age, MacLeish had much to say. Commenting on the scientific, political, and social developments between 1920 and 1960—from nuclear missiles, to the rise of nations, to the imbalance of power in the world—MacLeish observed that the greatest effect has been on man himself: "Our crisis, is man, the new man in whom knowledge is carried—along with the old ignorance which was there before: the new scientific man who knows but does not know, who can but can't, who will but won't—and who is dangerous to himself and others because he has lost his relation to his own reality in losing his relation to a world he thought he knew."

MacLeish felt that man faced a major problem in learning to

live with these discordant elements. Man has learned much about the universe but nothing about himself. The old relation between man and his world has been replaced by a new, precise, objective, dispassionate observation of the world. All this knowledge seems to exist of itself and not in human terms because "the knowledge of the fact has somehow come loose from the feel of the fact." For the first time in human history it is possible to know as a mind what cannot be comprehended as a man. MacLeish suggested that poetry could project an image for our time, could offer a means "by which life is apprehended as something to be felt and experienced rather than manipulated." Poetry, as he had said before, offered a means by which men could recognize themselves.[16]

IV *The Abuses of Poetry*

From the early 1920's MacLeish has castigated the literary time servers, both the imaginative writers and the critics who have made a business of literature. His main objection to these functionaries is that they have added to the confusions of the time.

He deplored the inadequacies of Realism, the prevailing mode of the 1920's; and he scored the novelists who used "the manner and method of realism to create a sordid, cynical, and unlovely society." They substituted Silenus for Faust, and they resorted to the literary devices of irony and pathos rather than to their own intuitive understanding of experience.[17] Within a few months of this rebuke of novelists and poets, MacLeish and his friend Lawrence Mason aimed their barbs at philosophic abstractions and published a hoax about a certain Peter Sczornik, a Czech scholar and purportedly a philosopher of grammar.[18]

MacLeish widened his target later in the decade when he wrote of novelists and poets who were in "the literature business," writers who contrived entertainment for readers and publicity for themselves. He observed the new literary type that had emerged from this artificial writing, "the couturier as critic," "the mannequin of books" whose job it was to promote fads and celebrities. He was concerned about the harm such a system would have on a genuine creative artist who must work in private to work honestly.[19] He later commented on the disproportionate emphasis on criticism: "a critic-ridden land like America where, for each page of creative writing, there are pounds of comment."[20] He explained that there is a difference between comment and criticism. The function of the critic he likened to the ribbed wheel on binoculars which holds in place an object otherwise blurred; interpretation may be vain but recognition possible.[21] MacLeish paid special tribute to Marguerite Caetani and the thirteen-year-old *Botteghe Oscure* which ceased publication in 1960, having never exceeded five thousand subscriptions. Though it appeared in Rome, it was an international publication. Dedicated to literature, it gave writers an opportunity to find one another, not personally but spiritually. MacLeish pointed out that it provided the kind of relationship that serious writers must find in order to continue to work and to develop.[22]

As already indicated MacLeish disliked the sickly introspection of the late nineteenth-century British poets just as he later deplored the contrived literary vogues that failed to provide the image appropriate for the time. Poetry, at its best, is always a search for the universal, not an exploitation of the personal. In *The Hamlet of A. MacLeish* he rebelled against the practice of exposing one's private sorrows for money and fame, of "making a business of despair" for critics to evaluate according to their standards of literary style.

As an example of exploitation of self, he referred to W. H. Auden and his imitators. This Eliot school of poets had turned attention inward and had helped delay the return of poetry to the whole experience. Their poetic language is "the living language at its most banal and deadened phrases. They have created from this stereotyped language a satiric, and sometimes a lyric poetry of great power." But the meanings are "inward toward the private reference of the poet."[23]

As another example of exploiting the self, he identified the "victim hero" as one of the false images created by writers who mirrored their own weaknesses. He deplored this romantic self-immolation that represented a kind of childish escapism. The truth they told was a truth "discreditable to the teller and the hearer" because it was "the low-down, the confession, the exposure."[24] In *Actfive* he describes this "victim hero" as one of the images worshiped by the American people in the years after World War II. He further commented on the immaturity of the modern "disillusioned hero" who fails to be a tragic figure because he lacks the capacity to "taste at the same time the possibility of human happiness." As he said in his essay on

Keats, "it is only when the two are known together in a single knowledge that either can be known."[25]

He observed the way in which Americans turn everything into a vogue—even art, "which should be the greatest destroyer of fashions." At one and the same time everyone reads James, then Joyce, then Eliot, or Kafka; then he reads the Communists one decade, the homosexuals another, "until the new writing begins to sound like the advertizing patter in the smart magazines." The young writers, hoping to be initiated into life and art in San Francisco, could not have chosen a worse place: "a cult in which Bohemianism itself is stereotyped and you can't even be a bum without bad liquor, boring sexuality, and the regulation beard." Their work, he observed, reflected their "initiation."[26]

MacLeish even rebuked Nobel prize-winner William Faulkner for joining the army of literary sex peddlers and for adding his contribution to false images. In the poem, "The Ballad of the Corn-Cob and the Lie," MacLeish seems to imply that Faulkner's deceitful image in *Sanctuary* set a dangerous pattern. There almost seems to be an analogy between the "rape" of the maiden and the deceptive tactics of the McCarthyites that "raped" the country in the early 1950's. These are the final lines:

> The impotent that could not—
> That leared with letching eye,
> They've learned to rape the country
> With a corn-cob and a lie.[27]

In an America where everything can be made a vogue, even the term "revolt" has become a fad. MacLeish frequently commented upon the difference between genuine poetic revolt that broke down conventions and a kind of literary one that assumed the proportion of a vogue. Apropos of the French philosophers and the American beatniks, he wrote: "It may perhaps astonish us that the age of technological triumph should have produced the Nausea of Sartre, the Absurd of Camus and the papal pronouncement that the earth was created to be a cemetery—to say nothing of the pronouncements of our own literary Halloweeners who play trick-or-treat with the writers of San Francisco and New York." True revolt is not "philosophical dissent." MacLeish found the revolt of Sartre, Malraux, and Camus "a pale and intellectual affair" beside the true revolt of Rimbaud. Apropos of the current philosophical view of life as absurd, and of the novels of Camus and Sartre, he wrote, "If everything is absurd, revolt against everything is absurd too and so is a novel about revolt."[28]

V Poetry and Experience (1961)

In the critical essays which make up *Poetry and Experience* MacLeish is concerned with the "means to meaning in poetry" and with the way in which four poets use these means to convey their interpretation of experience. The discussions always begin with the poems themselves, not with a theory. MacLeish differs from certain academic critics in that he considers a poem a re-creation of experience and not an intellectual exercise.

The Chinese military man and poet, Lu Chi, said, "Taking his position at the hub of things [the poet] contemplates the mystery of the universe." MacLeish restates Lu Chi's metaphor in this way: "The poet's labor is to struggle with the meaninglessness and silence of the world until he can force it to mean: until he can make the silence answer and the non-being BE." This Eastern idea differs radically from the Western one which describes a poet as "a man lost in himself... not capable of outward vision but only of inward." MacLeish quotes Sir Herbert Read who described the creation of a poem as "a passive waiting for the symbol to emerge from the depths of the unconscious."

MacLeish illustrates how Dylan Thomas' poem "Do Not Go Gentle from that Good Night" was able to "carry world across into the mind *whole*." The poem catches momentarily an experience whose meaning cannot be extracted, but can be felt by the emotions. This deceptively simple structure of imperative and declarative statements has within it another structure which the words as sounds make. MacLeish questions the extent to which Mallarmé insisted that poetry is made of words as sounds, not words as ideas. He compares his extreme position with that of the academic critic who believes that "words may be used as to be stripped clean of every association and effect *except* their 'meanings,' thus becoming intellectual symbols as precise and as sterilized as the symbols of mathematicians." He disproved Mallarmé's theory with a quotation from James Joyce's *Finnegan's Wake,* a deliberate experiment in word sounds but one that does correlate meanings and sounds.

George Moore, another theorist, tried to prove in the

anthology *Pure Poetry* that poetry was made up of words signifying things rather than sounds. MacLeish illustrates the close relationships of sound and meaning by showing the ugliness of a translation of a Mallarmé sonnet whose own words make "pure shape in the ear"; the reader "descends ... to the deliberate harshness of a literal paraphrase." The structure of meaning is as subtly controlled as the structure of sound because what is meant is something that is not entirely sayable. Sound in poetry is not mere embellishment or music; it has a structure of its own. He illustrates from several poems—a Shakespearean sonnet, a Herrick lyric, Pound's "Hugh Selwyn Mauberley"—that sound and meaning are inextricably woven to achieve a meaning, which, because of their interrelationships, can be felt rather than analyzed. It is the power of poetry to say what the reader has "known before" but in such a way that "he must *feel* it, *face* it, *live* it."

MacLeish makes several interesting comments about images, metaphors, and symbols. Because Chinese poets use images in a laconic and explicit way and without the usual tools of syntax, the juxtaposition of images is particularly striking. Images must work as images. By their unusual relationship they evoke recognition, an awareness, a glimpse into experience that the reader had previously known but had not fully realized. It is to the images, beautiful or not, that the emotions respond. Although MacLeish develops the idea about "the power of imagery to contain emotion" from his study of Chinese poetry, he turns to Marvell and to ancient British lyrics to illustrate how emotion is held between images. An emotional response is not achieved by description but by indirection: "By *not* speaking of it. By *not* speaking of it at all. By speaking of something else.... By leaving a space between one sensed image and another where what cannot be said can *be*."

MacLeish raises the interesting question whether coupled images which evoke a feeling do, in fact, discover a further meaning, not in the mind, which cannot understand, but in the emotion, which can. Among the poets who recognized the perceptive power of the imagination to bring "the whole soul of man into activity," Baudelaire described the poetic imagination as "the most scientific of all faculties because it alone comprehends 'the universal analogy.'" Wordsworth also described this art of relating the unrelated as "the pleasure which the mind derives from the perceptions of similitude in dissimilitude." MacLeish reiterates the point that the greater significance of coupled images is, therefore, "to comprehend an instant of the *analogie universelle*."

Comprehending the universal analogy makes sense of experience "in its *own* terms, not in terms of an equation of abstractions on a blackboard or a philosophy of abstractions in a book." Poetry gives meaning to fragments of experience by relating the parts to each other and to the whole, by showing that there is extraordinary truth to be seen, sensed, and felt in the fragments themselves. MacLeish turns to two poems, one by Baudelaire and one by Donne, to illustrate the idea that the universal analogy is sometimes so unbearable that only tough-minded poets and tough-minded readers are able to face up to it. In the Baudelaire poem "*Une Charogne*" (A Carcass, A Carrion), "death and sexuality are coupled in the incongruous congruity of panting lasciviousness and heaving putrescence." Donne in "The Relic" couples the incongruous in "A bracelet of bright hair about the bone."

MacLeish believes that the coupling of images, the relating of the incongruous, is a more characteristic means to meaning than is symbol. Coleridge wrote that "a symbol is characterized by a translucence of the special in the particular, or of the general in the special, or of the universal in the general: above all by the translucence of the eternal through and in the temporal." MacLeish points out that the definition implies two images and that it is the relationship that is the symbol. With symbols, the relationship is one of congruity; with coupled images, it is incongruity. In the symbol, the one "thing" is in front and the other behind: in coupled images, they stand side by side.

The second part of this valuable book, *Poetry and Experience*, is called "The Shape of Meaning." It makes a careful study of four major and quite dissimilar poets to discover the meaning each gives to experience—The Private World: Poems of Emily Dickinson; The Public World: Poems of Yeats; The Anti-World: Poems of Rimbaud; The Arable World: Poems of Keats.

A careful reading in the private world of Emily Dickinson will dispel any idea that these are simple poems and will indicate how comprehensive was her deliberate use of "the double structure of words as sounds and words as meanings." Her use of objects as abstractions, "presented for the eye to see and the ear to hear and the hand to touch," offers a difficulty to the reader. Another problem lies in the transparency of these objects, in the kind of coupling which MacLeish has called symbol. "When a poet commits himself to the private world... his own delights and dreads and fearful hopes and hopeless despairs, his *voice*... is more pervasive of his poems" than if his poems were from a public world. He is the actor, the observer, the one who suffers and who takes delight.

The Emily Dickinson "voice" which MacLeish discovers in her poems is one of restraint, of quietness; it is without self-pity. In her constant writing of death, grief, despair, agony, or fear, there is a note of gayety, even at her own expense. She always speaks to the reader, never to herself; her voice is never overheard, not in one of hundreds of poems discovered after her death. Her poems give to the reader "experience itself presented as *recognizable* experience." Her particular voice can compel a familiar experience "almost to *happen*." MacLeish found in her poetry the belief that the world is capable of meaning; he found in them Baudelaire's *analogie universelle*. Emily Dickinson does not assert the meaning of the universe, but she seizes upon the experience and holds it long enough to turn it true.

MacLeish, before turning to the public world of Yeats, made the point that all great poetry moved in the world of politics and in the out-of-doors; he cited as examples the poetry of Greece and of Shakespeare, Shelley, Goethe, and Rimbaud. Although men of the mid-twentieth century live a more public life than ever, and worry about mankind's soul but not their own, about public honesty, public disaster, and public leadership—these same men believe that poetry belongs indoors.

Responsibilities, published when Yeats was almost fifty, gives meaning to the public world. Two poems, "September 1913" and "Easter 1916," are not only bitter indictments of the Dubliners but give "a meaning in terms of human life, human history—the tragedy of the heart." "To a Shade" is addressed to Parnell, defeated by slanders of reactionaries in church and business; the "old foul mouth," one of the pack, was generally known. The poem, "The Grey Rock," may be called the key to Yeats's renunciation of the esthetes of the 1890's who made of art a "terrible goddess" but from whom he had learned his craft. Yeats realized that he had failed to "fight *as poet*... had lacked the strength to live while others were dying... had chosen the other, easier alternative." Yeats, as evidenced from *Responsibilities*, made no distinction between poetry and politics.

Arthur Rimbaud revolted against the world and expressed disgust for man and for God. It was "not only the passion of Rimbaud's disillusionment with life which makes the greatness of his poetry a challenge" but his concept of the poet as "truly the thief of fire," a kind of Prometheus contesting the higher power. Rimbaud believed that the poet should make himself a seer by "a persistent, enormous, planned disordering of all the senses—every form of love, of suffering, of madness... by this means he will arrive at the *Unknown*." Though his life as a poet was concentrated in less than five years, he left one of the most amazing poems the world has known—"*Bateau Ivre*" (Drunken Boat). The poem gives reality and life to the theory of disordered senses just as his letters on the same topic give only the descriptions.

MacLeish contrasts Baudelaire, who believed that the poet should discover the unknown through sensuous experience but who did not live his theory, with Rimbaud whose orgies with his poet-friend Verlaine make sordid history. His corruption was his own choice; his perversions, deliberate. Whatever the life and pretensions of Rimbaud, MacLeish richly illustrates the point that the poems are not the usual descriptions of visions: "They *are* the visions themselves: the images and rhythms and dislocations in which the visions present themselves. They are actions, poetic actions, moving with the timeless, effortless rapidity of the vision itself, not the ordered time, the rationalized time, of the vision remembered. Their end and aim is the end and aim of *vision*—to see the unseeable: not the end and aim of *literature*—to represent it." MacLeish sees in Rimbaud "the heroic and the tragic figure," one who did not reject the possibility of the world as have Camus and Sartre, leaders of the "literary revolt," but one who, after defeat and humiliation, could write, "It shall be lawful to me to possess the truth in one body and one soul."

In writing about "The Arable World" of John Keats, MacLeish points out that he, like Rimbaud, whose life and work were also abbreviated, has outlived the biased and ignorant evaluations of his contemporaries. MacLeish believes that "Keats had a truer sense of the tragic than any English poet since Shakespeare and precisely because he took a sharper delight in the loveliness of the world.... To taste the human tragedy one must taste at the same time the possibility of human happiness, for it is only when the two are known together in a single knowledge that either one can be known."

"Ode to a Nightingale" is a dramatic account of the perception of what it is "to fall too far into happiness," to be so in love with beauty as to long to escape the mortal world. MacLeish wrote that "a poem is not the perfected expression of a predetermined thought but is itself the process of its thinking moving from perception to perception, sense to sense; and in none of Keats's poems is the living process more alive than it is here." Man's realization of what it is to come into the presence of beauty of the world—comparable to the recognition scene in a play—is that "it cannot be possessed beyond the limits of space and time because the listener cannot be there to possess it." Keats recognized the peril of pursuing beauty too long and too far and of the danger of being led beyond the human world.

MacLeish describes "Ode on a Grecian Urn" as a "drama of perceptions" and calls attention to the many weighty opinions given to the last eighteen words on beauty and truth:

> Beauty is truth, truth beauty,—that is all
> Ye know on earth, and all ye need to know.

As MacLeish reads the poem, with its insistent image of excess of happiness, life in an eternity of the imagination is less than perfect. As MacLeish restates the resolution, the terms "beauty" and "truth" are essential: "To live only in the imagination, only in the eternal present which the imagination can impose upon the flowing away of time, is to abandon and leave deserted the human world." The "beauty" of time, of experience, of the "arable field of events" must be accepted along with the "truth" of eternities which the imagination can preserve.

Poetry and Experience is an important contribution to the study of poetry, a refreshing departure from the overwritten analyses which bury a poet's few disciplined lines in pages of literary exegesis. Gay Wilson Allen called the book "a serious and provocative contribution to the theory of poetry, an impressive effort by the poet, scholar and man of the world to find a meaningful relation between the poet and the world."[29]

CHAPTER *8*

The Poet's Work

ARCHIBALD MacLEISH was first represented in the *Yale Literary Magazine*, October, 1911, by the poem, "Gifts." *Poetry and Experience* was published in 1961. During the half-century between the two dates more revolutionary changes took place, not only in man's knowledge of the world but in his way of life—economic, social, political—than in any other span of fifty years in recorded human history. To find similarities at the beginning and at the end of this period is to find the exception and not the rule. Although man's *modus vivendi* has seemingly changed, many of his patterns of thought belong to the time before World War I. The effect of these cataclysmic changes upon man as a human being has become one of the central problems of our time.

MacLeish has been aware of the discrepancies between the way man lives and the way he thinks and also of the antiquated ideas that prevent his living intelligently in the modern technological world. To attempt to give meaning to life at a time when the abstractions of science and philosophy and politics dominate man's thinking is to seek continually the living image that will most completely crystallize the chaotic world of man's experience. MacLeish has been concerned with the present, with the special and changing quality that seems to predominate in each decade; he has sought to invent the appropriate metaphor for the time and has urged that his fellow poets do the same. In both prose and verse he has written about outworn dogmas and conventions that turn man's thought and life back rather than direct them forward. From the time of his Paris sojourn, he has persistently sought a pattern of thought appropriate to the new world. Firm in his belief that man can achieve a good life in a democracy, he has directed his attention to the positive, the constructive, and the idealistic in order to suggest ways in which man can best fulfill himself in a world that requires a new mode of thinking.

Because he has often written with candor, he has brought himself into sharp conflict with those who are partisan in politics, orthodox in religion, and dogmatic in art. Having determined that it is the role of the poet to concentrate upon the essential nature of the time, he has continued—in spite of criticism—to seek the metaphor appropriate for his age.

From the beginning his work reveals a consistent honesty with himself, a courage to express an opinion not likely to be popular, a readiness to stand by principle when the prevailing thought is otherwise. His work indicates that he often anticipated the modes of thought of the several decades in which he wrote rather than reflected them. His independent cast of mind often placed him among the forerunners rather than with the rear guard. From the early poems of his undergraduate years to the lyrics written in the 1950's, from the tentative dramatic scenes to the fully developed plays, from the early statements about American character to the appraisal of the race situation in Mississippi, from the early theories of poetry and the poet's role to the fully defined expression of the later years, MacLeish has shown growth and increasing strength. A considerable body of work, it makes a significant statement about the place of the poet and of poetry in American life.

Through his own poetry, his articles on poetry, and through his prose, MacLeish has exemplified his own thesis that to be a poet is to be a man. Gifted with a fine lyric talent, disciplined to write in delicate imagery and a musical line of many patterns, and strengthened through repeated conflict on controversial issues, he has emerged as a major figure on the American literary scene. He has made a contribution to American poetry, and he has also given a sense of direction to American life. During the war years he had the qualities that the time of crisis demanded; he set aside his first love, poetry, to serve his country and risked irreparable damage to his chosen work and its development; however, he returned to poetry and proved that public service and lyric expression are not incompatible.

MacLeish speaks with many voices. There is the delicate insight into human relationship, the robust humor at folly and pretension, the outspoken anger over deceit or treachery or injustice, the compassion for the suffering of others, the forthright candor toward conventional and outmoded beliefs. Through plays, poetry, and prose, he continues to speak to an increasing audience, to make his own poetry as much of the integral part of life as possible. He continues to speak and to write on the current scene, a man aware of his own time. He is obviously seeking to follow his own advice:

> Poets, deserted by the world before,
> Turn round into the actual air:
> Invent the age! Invent the metaphor!

Notes and References

Chapter One

1. Archibald MacLeish, "Poetry and the Public World," *The Atlantic*, CLXIII (June, 1939), 829-30. Reprinted in *A Time to Speak*.
2. *Idem.*, "The Poet and the Press," *The Atlantic*, CCIII (March, 1959), 46. Originally delivered as the Gideon Seymour Lecture at the University of Minnesota. See also Archibald MacLeish, "Portrait of a Yankee Skipper," *American Heritage*, VIII (December, 1956), 38-43 ff.
3. *Idem.*, "On the Teaching of Writing," *Harper's*, CCXIX (October, 1959), 160.

Chapter Two

1. Archibald MacLeish, *The Tower of Ivory*, with a Foreword by Lawrence Mason (New Haven, 1917).
2. *Parabalou*, Issued by the Publisher from Will Warren's Den, Farmington, Connecticut. No. 1, 1920; No. 2, 1920; No. 3, 1921.
3. Northrop Frye, *Fearful Symmetry* (Princeton, 1947), pp. 61 ff.
4. R. P. Blackmur, "A Modern Poet in Eden," *Poetry*, XXVIII (September, 1926), 339 ff.
5. Llewellyn Jones, "A. MacLeish: a Modern Metaphysicist," *English Journal*, XXIV (June, 1935), 443.
6. For an illustration of the Laforgue technique, see the translation of the monologue of Laforgue's "Hamlet," Arthur Symons, *The Symbolist Movement in Literature* (New York, 1919, 1958) (A Dutton Paperback), p. 58.
7. Pound seems to have felt that the epigraph gave a poem a special tone. He is said to have recommended that Eliot change the epigraph originally heading *The Waste Land* to a quotation from Dante.
8. Sir James Frazer, *The Golden Bough*, one-volume edition (New York, 1958), Chapter 29.
9. See Warren Ramsay, *Jules Laforgue and the Ironic Inheritance* (New York, 1953), pp. 202 ff. He defines Laforgue as an impressionist rather than a symbolist.
10. The use of colloquial speech, a technique imitated by other poets, Eliot is supposed to have learned from Laforgue.
11. See the discussion of *"Une Charogne"* by Baudelaire in Archibald MacLeish, *Poetry and Experience* (Boston, 1961), pp. 70 ff.
12. Morton Zabel, "The Compromise of A. MacLeish," *Poetry*, XXXVI (August, 1930), 272.
13. I. L. Solomon, "A Peacemaker," *Saturday Review*, XXXV (December 27, 1952), 18.
14. Amos Wilder, *The Spiritual Aspects of the New Poetry* (New York, 1940), p. 99.
15. Frederick J. Hoffman, *The Twenties* (New York, 1955), pp. 287-88.
16. George Dangerfield, "Archibald MacLeish: An Appreciation," *The Bookman*, LXXII (January, 1931), 495.

17. For translations of the Laforgue "Hamlet" see Arthur Symons, *op. cit.*, and Oscar Cargill, *Intellectual America* (New York, 1941), pp. 208 ff. For a discussion of Laforgue's interest in psychology see Ramsay, *op. cit.* See entries under Hartmann.

18. Wilder, *op. cit.*, pp. 75, 102-3, 76.

19. A number of critics have found echoes of St.-John Perse in the poems of MacLeish. *Anabase* was published in France, 1925. T. S. Eliot, in his introduction to his translation, *Anabasis* (New York, 1938, 1949) says, "The poem is a series of images of migration, of conquest of vast spaces of Asiatic wastes, of destruction and foundation of cities and civilizations of any races or epochs of the ancient East." It is a chronical of the ascent of a Conqueror—the Stranger—from the seashore to the deserts of Central Asia, the foundation of a city, the restlessness which follows, the schemes of further conquest, the arrival, the repose, and the continued urge toward other conquests. Though written as prose, it has the essential qualities of lyric poetry: the unusual imagery, a juxtaposition of unexpected images that intimates rather than expresses meaning, the unmistakable qualities of sound and rhythm. The "action" concerns the conditions of men—all men—in their ways and manners, recorded without historical or ideological allusions. By dispensing with the usual links and descriptive or explanatory matter, St.-John Perse has heightened the intensity of expression. It is a poem derived from experience rather than literature, a poem close to the elemental lives of peoples still primitive.

20. Jessie L. Weston, *From Ritual to Romance* (Doubleday Anchor Book) (New York, 1957), p. 203.

21. About the autobiographical nature of these lines see "Fragments of a Biography," *The American Caravan*, ed. Van Wyck Brooks, *et al.* (New York, 1927).

22. Ramsay, *op. cit.*, p. 157.

23. Mason Wade, "The Anabasis of A. MacLeish," *North American Review*, CCXLIII (Summer, 1937), 339.

24. Dangerfield, *op. cit.*, p. 495.

25. Rica Brenner, *Poets of Our Time* (New York, 1941), p. 71.

26. Lewis Galantière, "Hamlet for Our Time," *The Nation*, CXXVIII (April 17, 1929), 471.

27. Hayden Carruth, "MacLeish's Poetry," *The Nation*, CLXXVI (January 31, 1953), 103.

28. Solomon, *op. cit.*, p. 19.

29. Richard Eberhart, "The Pattern of MacLeish's Poetry," New York *Times Book Review*, November 23, 1952.

30. Kimon Friar, "The Poet of Action," *New Republic*, CXXVII (December 15, 1952), 20.

Chapter Three

1. Archibald MacLeish, ".... and Apple Pie," *Fortune*, I:2 (March, 1930), 91.

2. *Idem.*, "Skyscrapers," *Fortune*, II:1 (July, 1930), 34.

3. *Idem.*, "The Case Against Roosevelt," *Fortune*, XII:6 (December, 1935), 102.

4. Morton Zabel, *op. cit.*, p. 274.

5. Alfred Kreymborg, "The Moon is Dead," *The Saturday Review of Literature*, X (January 27, 1934), 435.

6. Jones, *op. cit.*, p. 450.

7. Archibald MacLeish, "Nevertheless One Debt," *Poetry*, XXXVIII (July, 1931), 209. Reprinted in *A Time to Speak*.

8. Dangerfield, *op. cit.*, pp. 494, 493.

9. Imagery in the poem perhaps reflects the poet's visit to Persia during his years in France. For a discussion of "You, Andrew Marvell," see Laurence Perrine, *Sound and Sense* (New York, 1956, 1963), pp. 68-69.

10. Zabel, *op. cit.*, p. 273.

11. Robert Penn Warren, "Twelve Poets," *American Review*, III (March, 1934), 217.

12. MacLeish, *op. cit.*, p. 215. It may be worth noting that this statement of belief in the common man was written before the election of President Roosevelt.

13. MacLeish explained the source he used and the perspective taken. See *The Complete Poems 1917-1952* (Boston, 1952), pp. 325-26.

14. Dante Alighieri, *The Divine Comedy*, John D. Sinclair, Trans., (New York, 1961), pp. 326-27.

15. For an insight into the way in which the poet made use of his historical source, compare chapter forty of *The Discovery and Conquest of Mexico 1517-1521* by Bernal Díaz del Castillo and the sixth book of *Conquistador*.

16. Edmund Wilson, "The Omelet of A. MacLeish," *The New Yorker*, XIX (January 14, 1939), 23, parodies the mannered use of the colon, the broken line, the adaptation of the terza rima, and the rhetorical quality of some of the lines. In a curious early piece in which MacLeish collaborated with Lawrence Mason, "The Next Philosophy," *North American Review*, CCXVII (May, 1923), 698 ff., the writers apparently contrived a hoax about a Czech, Peter Sczornik, and his philosophy of grammar, the universal solvent. They made a fetish of the colon, as for instance, God: the Copula, or Immortality: the Infinitive. See "Notebooks 1924-1938," *Poetry*, LXXIII (October, 1948), 40. Morton Zabel, in an angry rebuttal about a group of polemical essays by MacLeish, "The Poet on Capitol Hill," *Partisan Review*, VIII (February, 1941), 145, reports his exhaustive and unsuccessful search for the identity of this Czech philosopher. Taking the article seriously, he saw in it a psychological study of the poet's mind.

17. Eda Lou Walton, "Archibald MacLeish," *The Nation*, CXXXVIII (January 10, 1934), 48.

18. Warren, *op. cit.*, p. 215.

19. Solomon, *op. cit.*, p. 19.

20. S. F., "Escape to the Past," *New Masses*, VIII-IX (July, 1932), 26.

21. For a discussion of the Battle of Radio City, the strength and the weakness of "Mankind at the Crossroads," the fresco which was destroyed at the request of the Rockefellers, see Frank Jewett Mather, Sr., "Rivera's American Murals," *The Saturday Review of Literature*, X (May 19, 1934), 697-99.

22. Archibald MacLeish, "Public Speech and Private Speech in Poetry," *The Yale Review*, XXVII (March, 1938), 541.

23. Michael Gold, "Out of the Fascist Unconscious," *New Republic*, LXXV (July 26, 1933), 295.

24. William Rose Benét, "Round about Parnassus," *The Saturday Review of Literature*, X (July 29, 1933), 21.

25. Jones, *op. cit.*, p. 448.

26. For the controversy and the parodies of "Invocation to the Social Muse" see *New Republic*, LXXIII (December 14, 1932), 125-26; (February 8, 1933), 346-48.

27. Archibald MacLeish, "The Social Cant," *New Republic*, LXXIII (December 21, 1933), 156-58.

28. *Idem.*, "The Poetry of Karl Marx," *The Saturday Review of Literature*, X (February 17, 1934), 485-86.

29. *Ibid.*, p. 486.

30. Archibald MacLeish, "The Tradition of the People," *New Masses*, XX (September 1, 1936), 26. Review of Carl Sandburg's *The People Yes*; reprinted as "Mr. Sandburg and the Doctrinaires," in *A Time to Speak*.

31. Benét, *op. cit.*, p. 21.

32. Kreymborg, *op. cit.*, p. 435.

33. Warren, *op. cit.*, pp. 212-18.

34. Walton, *op. cit.*, pp. 48-49.

35. Conrad Aiken, "Development of a Poet," *New Republic*, LXXVII (January 17, 1934), 287.

36. Morton Zabel, "Comment—Cinema of Hamlet," *Poetry*, XLIV (June, 1934), 150-59.

37. R. P. Blackmur, "Mr. MacLeish's Predicament," *American Mercury*, XXXI (April, 1934), 507-8.

38. C. G. Poore, "Poems 1924-1933," New York *Times Book Review*, February 4, 1934.

Chapter Four

1. Archibald MacLeish, "Public Speech and Private Speech in Poetry," *The Yale Review*, XXVII (March, 1938), 536-47. Reprinted in *A Time to Speak*.

2. *Idem.*, "Poetry and the Public World," *The Atlantic*, CLXIII (June, 1939), 825-30. Reprinted in *A Time to Speak*.

3. *Idem.*, "A Stage for Poetry," *Stage*, (November, 1935), Reprinted in *A Time to Speak* (Boston, 1940), p. 80.

4. Some of the essays which concern the alternative between material comforts or freedom are "The American Cause" (November 20, 1940), "Divided We Fall" (March 19, 1942), "The Act of Faith" (June, 1950), and "To Make Men Free" (November, 1951).

5. Joseph Wood Krutch, "Man's Fate," *The Nation*, CXL (March 21, 1935), 369-70.

6. Ashley Dukes, "The English Scene," *Theatre Arts*, XXI (February, 1937), 105.

7. Archibald MacLeish, "Munich and the Americans," *The Nation*, CXLVII (October 15, 1938), 370-71, discussed what Czechoslovakia meant to American isolationists, "indifferent to the issues."

8. Orrin E. Dunlop, "The Fall of the City," New York *Times*, April 18, 1937.

9. O. Larkin, "Air Waves and Sight Lines," *Theatre Arts*, XXII (December, 1938), 890.

10. Gilbert Seldes, "The People and the Arts," *Scribner's*, CI (June, 1937), 61-62.

11. Archibald MacLeish, "The War is Ours." *New Masses*, XXIII (June 22, 1937), 5. This address, which opened the National Congress of American Writers, was reprinted with the title "The Communists, the Writers, and the Spanish War" in *A Time to Speak*. MacLeish also wrote three articles, "Background for War." for *Fortune*. The second, "The Struggle in Spain" (XV [April, 1937], 81 ff.), concerned the history of Spain during the last two centuries and the attempt of the people to free themselves from their feudal past, and the domination of church, landowners, and army.

12. "Interview with MacLeish recorded by Orrin E. Dunlop, Jr.," New York *Times*, October 30, 1938.

13. "Air Raid," *Time*, XXXII (October 31, 1938), 30.

14. "Land of the Free," *Christian Century*, LV (April 13, 1938), 455.

15. "Talking Pictures," *Time*, XXXI (April 25. 1938), 69.

16. Richard Eberhart, "The Pattern of MacLeish's Poetry," New York *Times Book Review*, November 23, 1952.

17. J. M. Brinnin, "For a Wider Audience," *Poetry* (April, 1940), 45.

18. "Interview with Orrin E. Dunlop, Jr.," New York *Times*, April 21, 1940.

19. Archibald MacLeish, "The Isolation of the American Artist," *The Atlantic*, CCI (January, 1958), 58.

Chapter Five

1. For a description of the range and difficulty of the assignment, see Amy Loveman, "A Poet in Government," *The Saturday Review of Literature*, XXIV (November 1, 1941), 10; James Reston, "Defense Picture Given to World in All Media by Federal Agencies," New York *Times*, October 27, 1941.

2. Archibald MacLeish, *American Opinion and the War* (Rede Lecture, Cambridge University, 1942) (Cambridge, 1942).

3. In one record of the period, Robert E. Sherwood, *Roosevelt and Hopkins* (New York, 1948), the name of Archibald MacLeish appears only twice.

4. Coleman Rosenberger, "Poets and Politicians," *Poetry*, LXV (March, 1945), 322-27, comments on the public men throughout history who have been poets. His recording of the greeting-card jingles that appear copiously in the *Congressional Record* are a sad comment on the quality of some American Congressmen.

5. Archibald MacLeish, "A Poet Speaks from the Visitor's Gallery," *The New Yorker*, XIX (September 11, 1945), 30.

6. "Report of the Chairman of the Program Coordinating Committee, Archibald MacLeish, to the Conference, Paris, December 9, 1946," *International Conciliation*, CCCCXXXI (May, 1947), 304-16, New York, Carnegie Endowment for International Peace.

7. "M'Leish is Chosen for Library Post," New York *Times*, June 7,

1939; "M'Leish Assailed in Debate in House," New York *Times,* June 8, 1939. J. Parnell Thomas (Rep., N. J.) called MacLeish a "Fellow Traveler" and Sam Rayburn resented the attack.

8. Congressman Thomas resigned from his seat in the House, January 2, 1950, after having been sentenced for six to eighteen months in prison and fined $10,000 for defrauding the Government. He had been taking "salary kickbacks" from non-working employees on his Congressional payroll. See entries in the 1949 *Index* to the New York *Times.*

9. See "A Poet for Librarian" (editorial), New York *Times,* June 8, 1939, and "Letters to the Times," June 15, 1939; "Panned Poet," *Newsweek,* XIII (June 19, 1939), 20; "Poet in Washington," *New Republic,* XCIX (June 21, 1939), 171.

10. "Letters to the Times," New York *Times,* June 15, 1939; July 15; July 24; July 26.

11. M. Llewellyn Raney, "The MacLeish Case," *Library Journal,* LXIV (July, 1939), 522; "Appointment Endorsed by New York Public Library Staff Association," New York *Times,* June 15, 1939; "Appointment Endorsed by Metropolitan Library Council," New York *Times,* June 16, 1939.

12. "Library, Librarian," *Time,* XXXIII (June 19, 1939), 18; John Chamberlain, "Archibald MacLeish," *The Saturday Review of Literature,* XX (June 24, 1939), 10-11; "A Poet for Librarian," New York *Times,* June 8, 1939.

13. "MacLeish Confirmed," New York *Times,* June 30, 1939; "Librarian MacLeish," New York *Times,* July 1, 1939.

14. "Editorial Forum": "Putnam Praises MacLeish," *Library Journal,* LXIV (November 1, 1939), 863.

15. Mildred Adams, "Two Men and Five Million Books," New York *Times Magazine,* October 29, 1939; see also the editorial, "Librarian Mac-Leish," New York *Times,* March 30, 1940.

16. Archibald MacLeish, "The Reorganization of the Library of Congress, 1939-1944," *Library Quarterly,* XIV (October, 1944), 279.

17. "Salaries Held Too Small," letter from Archibald MacLeish to the New York *Times,* April 19, 1940; "The Underpaid Librarian," editorial in the New York *Times,* April 21, 1940.

18. H. C. Shriver and C. Larson, "Archibald MacLeish's Two Years as Librarian," *The Saturday Review of Literature,* XXIV (October 18, 1941), 10-11.

19. Herbert Lyons, Jr., "Front-Line Librarian," New York *Times Magazine,* June 29, 1941.

20. "War Peril to Lore Arouses Scholars," New York *Times,* January 27, 1940.

21. See MacLeish, *Library Quarterly,* XIV (October, 1944), 279 for chart which shows the plan of organization, division of responsibilities, and the range of activities of the Library of Congress and p. 305 for chart of the Reference Department.

22. Keyes D. Metcalf, "Editorial Forum," *Library Journal,* LXX (March 1, 1945), 213.

23. F. A. Mullen, "Reader's Open Forum," *Library Journal* LXX (April 15, 1945), 326.

24. Archibald MacLeish, "The Librarian and the Democratic Process," (May 31, 1940), reprinted in *A Time to Speak.*

25. *Idem.*, "Of the Librarian's Profession," *The Atlantic*, CLXV (June, 1940), 789-90. Reprinted in *A Time to Speak*. There are many repetitions of "the Word," a mannerism that Edmund Wilson was to mimic. See below, footnote number 30.

26. *Idem.*, "Librarians in the Contemporary Crisis," *Library Journal* LXIV (November 15, 1939), 879-92. Reprinted in *A Time to Speak*.

27. *Idem.*, "The Country of the Mind Must Also Attack," address delivered to the American Library Association, June 26, 1942. Reprinted in *A Time to Act*.

28. *Idem.*, "The Irresponsibles," *The Nation*, CL (May 18, 1940), 618-23. Reprinted in *A Time to Speak*.

29. *Ibid.*

30. *Idem.*, "Post-War Writers and Pre-War Readers," address delivered before the American Association for Adult Education, New York City, May 23, 1940. The speech was printed in the *New Republic*, CII (June 10, 1940), 789-90 because of the "partial and inadequate reports" given by the daily press which led to "bitter attacks" and "enthusiastic praise." Some measure of the response can be indicated by the letters and comments printed in the New York *Times*: May 25, May 26, May 26 (editorial), and May 28.

31. Edmund Wilson, "Archibald MacLeish and 'the Word,'" *New Republic*, CIII (July 1, 1940), 30-32.

32. Morton Zabel, "The Poet on Capitol Hill," *Partisan Review*, VIII (January, 1941), 1-17.

33. Burton Rascoe, "The Tough-Muscled Boys of Literature," *American Mercury*, LI (November, 1940), 369.

34. Archibald MacLeish, "Prophets of Disaster," *The Atlantic*, CLXVIII (October, 1941), 480. Address given at commencement, University of Pennsylvania, June 11, 1941, and reprinted under the title, "Prophets of Doom," by the University of Pennsylvania Press. Reprinted in *A Time to Act*.

35. *Idem.*, "The Power of the Book," address delivered before the American Booksellers Association, May 6, 1942. Reprinted in *A Time to Act*.

36. See "Liberalism and the Anti-Fascist Front," *Survey Graphic*, XXVIII (May, 1939), 321-23. Reprinted as "The Affirmation" in *A Time to Speak*. "The Image of Victory," *The Atlantic*, CLXX (July, 1942), 1-6.

37. "Liberalism and the Anti-Fascist Front," *op. cit.*, p. 321.

38. Archibald MacLeish, "The American Cause," address delivered at Faneuil Hall, Boston, November 20, 1940. This essay with another, "The American Mobilization," and a Foreword by the author was published under the title *The American Cause* (New York, 1941). Reprinted in *A Time to Act*.

39. *Idem.*, "Freedom to End Freedom," *Survey Graphic*, XXVIII (February, 1939), 29. Reprinted in *A Time to Speak*.

40. *Idem.*, "Divided We Fall," address delivered at the inauguration of Freedom House, March 19, 1942. Reprinted in *A Time to Act*.

41. *Idem.*, "The Responsibility of the Press," address delivered before the American Society of Newspaper Editors, April 17, 1942. Reprinted in *A Time to Act*.

42. *Idem.*, "To the Class of 1941," commencement address delivered at Union College, June 9, 1941. Reprinted in *A Time to Act*.

43. *Idem.*, "The Strategy of Truth," address delivered at the annual luncheon of the Associated Press, April 20, 1942. Reprinted in *A Time to Act.*

44. Seldon Rodman, "Twixt Pundit and Poet," *The Saturday Review of Literature*, XXXI (August 14, 1948), 29.

45. Peter Viereck, "Indignant Sing-Song," New York *Times Book Review*, November 21, 1948.

Chapter Six

1. See Chapter Seven, section two, "On the Nature of Communism," for a discussion of MacLeish's account of the hysteria of the 1950's. One representative strong statement is to be found in "The Revulsion of Decency," reprinted in *Freedom Is the Right to Choose*, (Boston, 1951), pp. 99 ff.

2. Charles Poore, "Books of the Times," New York *Times Book Review*, November 29, 1952.

3. Richard Eberhart, "The Pattern of MacLeish's Poetry," New York *Times Book Review*, November 23, 1952.

4. Solomon, *op. cit.*, pp. 18-19.

5. Carruth, *op. cit.*, p. 103.

6. Friar, *op. cit.*, pp. 19-20.

7. The image of the two trees appears in stanzas 1, 2, 21, and 25. The rest of the discussion follows, in order, the sequence between stanzas 3 and 28.

8. Sara Henderson Hay, "Fall to Divinity," *Saturday Review*, XXXVII (December 4, 1954), 28.

9. Randall Jarrell, "Recent Poetry," *The Yale Review*, XLIV (June, 1955), 602-3.

10. Richard Eberhart, "The More I Have Traveled," New York *Times Book Review*, October 10, 1954.

11. Archibald MacLeish, "The Poet as Playwright," *The Atlantic*, CXCV (February, 1955), 49-52.

12. For a discussion of The Book of Job, see A. B. Davidson and C. H. Toy, "Job," *Encyclopaedia Britannica* (11th edition, 1911).

13. For statements by the playwright about the relevance of the Job story to our time, see the Foreword by the Author in the Samuel French edition, reprinted from The New York *Times*. See also Archibald MacLeish, "The Book of Job," *Christian Century*, LXXVI (April 8, 1962), 419-22; interview with Jean White, of the Washington *Post and Times Herald*, November 30, 1958, reprinted in *Library Journal*, LXXXIV (January 1, 1959), 36-37.

14. The text followed in this discussion is the version originally published by Houghton Mifflin, 1958, except for references and a few lines quoted from the second act of the Broadway version published by Samuel French, Inc. A comparison of these two texts indicates the role played by a dynamic director and the changes made in the script during production. Many of the changes clarify ideas in the original version, but some of them also change the original concept. The original sequence of eleven scenes has been made into two acts, the first twice the length of the second. Lines which do not carry the movement of the play forward

have been cut; other lines, necessary to the meaning, have been repeated or added. A number of transitions have been more fully developed to clarify the introduction of new characters or the start of new scenes.

15. In the Broadway version Nickles slashes the tent ropes after the revelation of the murder of the youngest child, Rebecca. The tent wall collapses.

16. Dudley Fitts, "Affliction of a New Job," New York *Times Book Review*, March 23, 1958, wrote: "The most brilliant invention of the play is the covering device that sets everything in motion that provides a chorus for the action." The two masks "start a parody of the Passion of Job and suddenly find themselves involved beyond their depth in a real performance. The composition in these passages has pitch and force, far more tragic than anything that happens." Joseph Wood Krutch thought the masks were too much like Beckett's half-witted clowns. "Universe at Stage Center," *Theatre Arts*, XLII (August, 1958), 9-11.

17. In the Broadway version Nickles is described as a "bitter boy" or a child. Elia Kazan seemed to think of him as something of a Beatnik. See "The Staging of a Play," *Esquire*, LI (May, 1959), 144 ff. This article is made up of excerpts from the notebooks and letters between playwright and director during the Elia Kazan staging of *J. B.*

18. John Ciardi in "'J. B.' and Job," *Saturday Review*, XLI (March 8, 1958), 11-12, wrote that MacLeish's great technical achievement was his "forging of a true poetic stage line for our time."

19. This speech has been deleted from the Broadway version.

20. The original characterization of Nickles as "an honest, disillusioned man" sensitive to the suffering and injustice inflicted upon J. B. has been changed in the acting version; in it Nickles is a cynic who comments caustically on J. B.'s belief in himself and in God's justice. He is very closely connected with several catastrophes: he throws pop bottles to the messengers, the camera to the newsmen, police coats to the officers; he dances with the society editor.

21. John Ciardi in "'J. B.' Revisited," *Saturday Review*, XLIII (January 30, 1960), 39, questioned whether the Old Testament was the proper idiom "of star-blinded nothingness."

22. A number of critics reacted against J. B.'s insensitivity to so much ruthless destruction. Kenneth Tynan, "The Theatre," *The New Yorker*, XXXIV (December 20, 1958), 70-72, thought the sequence of catastrophes monotonous and for some curious reason "longed for a representative from a foreign culture"—Oriental preferably.

23. In the original version the scenes of the Godmask and the Satan-mask were usually separate. In the Broadway version their comments arise as if spontaneously from the misfortunes of J. B. and his family, or out of their own rivalry. As a result, the family seems to be even more the victims of a "spinning joke." In some of the scenes Mr. Zuss gives J. B. the cue, particularly when the banker hesitates on the Biblical lines. In much the same way "The Distant Voice" coaches Godmask on lines from the Book of Job, and the lines gain in emphasis from repetition. Act I of the Broadway version closes with the strong and repeated Biblical utterance of J. B., "Show me my guilt, O God!" rather than with Nickles' penetrating and embarrassing questions to Mr. Zuss.

24. The second act of the Broadway version opens with the two masks

in contest over dominating their victim. Nickles urges the women who survived the blast to show J. B. the pointlessness of his suffering, the indifference of the universe. The masks also identify the comforters before they enter, a detail omitted in the original.

25. The mutual hate of these three comforters, each of whom is jealous of his partial truth, is pointed up in the Broadway version by their argument about guilt. J. B. definitely rejects the answer each of the comforters has to offer. The sense of man's hopelessness in an indifferent universe is accentuated by several repetitions of the line, "And that is all."

26. Archibald MacLeish, "The Men Behind 'J. B.'," *Theatre Arts,* XLIII (April, 1959), 61-62; see also "Foreword by the Author," reprinted from the New York *Times,* Samuel French edition of *J. B.*

27. Charles A. Fenton, "Theatre," *The Nation,* CLXXXVI (May 10, 1958), 425-26.

28. Tom F. Driver, "Notable, Regrettable," *Christian Century,* LXXVI (January 7, 1959), 21-22.

29. Theodore A. Webb, "Letters to the Editor," *Christian Century,* LXXV (August 13, 1958), 926.

30. Samuel Terrien, "J. B. and Job," *Christian Century,* LXXVI (January 7, 1959), 9-11.

31. Henry P. Van Dusen, "Third Thoughts on 'J. B.'," *Christian Century,* LXXVI (January 28, 1959), 106-7.

32. Richard Hayes, "The Humanism of Crisis," *Commonweal,* LXX (May 8, 1959), 153-54.

33. Reinhold Niebuhr, "Three Opinions on 'J. B.'," *Life,* LVI (May 18, 1959), 135-37.

34. "The Staging of a Play," *Esquire,* LI (May, 1959), 156-57.

35. Brooks Atkinson, "Theatre: Archibald MacLeish's New Play, 'J. B.'," New York *Times,* April 24, 1958.

Chapter Seven

1. Archibald MacLeish, "Poetry and the Public World," *The Atlantic,* CLXIII (June, 1939), 829.

2. *Idem.,* "Notebooks, 1924-1933," *Poetry,* LXXIII (October, 1948), 40.

3. Robert Hillyer wrote two articles, "Treason's Strange Fruit," and "Poetry's New Priesthood," published in the June 11 and June 18, 1949, issues of *The Saturday Review of Literature.* Norman Cousins and Harrison Smith took full responsibility for starting a controversy over the articles. Malcolm Cowley, "Battle over Ezra Pound," *New Republic,* CXXL (October 3, 1949), 17 ff., wrote that Hillyer extended to national and international fields a personal grudge against Eliot and Pound. *The Nation,* CLXIX (December 17, 1949), 598-99, printed a letter to the editors of the *Saturday Review* signed by eighty-four academic and literary people calling Hillyer's methods "reprehensible" and the magazine's campaign "dangerous and unprincipled."

4. Archibald MacLeish, "In Praise of Dissent," New York *Times Book Review,* December 16, 1956.

5. *Idem.,* "The Conquest of America," *The Atlantic,* CLXXXIV (August, 1949), 18, 19.

6. *Idem.*, "The Act of Faith," *The Atlantic* CLXXXV (June, 1950), 31-34.

7. *Idem.*, "The Power of Choice," *The Atlantic*, CLXXXVIII (August, 1951), 44.

8. *Idem.*, "To Make Men Free," *The Atlantic*, CLXXXVIII (November, 1951), 27, 28, 30.

9. *Idem.*, "The Alternative," *The Yale Review*, XLIV (June, 1955), 481-96.

10. *Idem.*, "Why Must We Hate?" *The Atlantic*, CCII (February, 1963), 79-82.

11. *Idem.*, "The Muses' Sterner Laws," *New Republic*, CXXVIII (July 13, 1953), 16-18.

12. *Idem.*, "Changes in the Weather," *New Republic*, CXXXV (July 2, 1956), 16-18.

13. *Idem.*, "The Isolation of the American Artist," *The Atlantic*, CCI (January, 1958), 57, 59.

14. *Idem.*, "The Poet and the Press," *The Atlantic*, CCIII (March, 1959), 44, 46. Originally delivered as the Gideon Seymour Lecture at the University of Minnesota.

15. *Idem.*, "Why Do We Teach Poetry?" *The Atlantic*, CXCVII (March, 1956), 50, 51.

16. *Idem.*, "To Face the Real Crisis," New York *Times Magazine*, December 25, 1960.

17. *Idem.*, "New Age and New Writers," *The Yale Review*, XII (January, 1923), 317.

18. Archibald MacLeish and Lawrence Mason, "The Next Philosophy," *North American Review*, CCXVII (May, 1923), 698 ff.

19. Archibald MacLeish, "Behold the Critiquins," *The Saturday Review of Literature*, IV (January 21, 1928), 529.

20. *Idem.*, "A New Life of Melville," *Bookman*, LXIX (April, 1929), 183.

21. *Idem.*, "Amy Lowell and the Art of Poetry," *North American Review*, CCXXI (March, 1925), 508-21.

22. *Idem.*, "Requiem for a Literary Haven," *Saturday Review*, XLIII (November 26, 1960), 26.

23. *Idem.*, "Public Speech and Private Speech in Poetry," *The Yale Review*, XXVII (March, 1938), 547.

24. *Idem.*, "Prophets of Disaster," *The Atlantic*, LXVIII (October, 1941), 480.

25. *Idem.*, *Poetry and Experience* (Boston, 1961), pp. 177-78.

26. *Idem.*, "On the Teaching of Writing," *Harper's*, CCXIX (October, 1959), 161.

27. *Idem.*, *Collected Poems 1917-1952*, (Boston, 1952), p. 161.

28. *Idem.*, *Poetry and Experience*, (Boston, 1961), pp. 150, 151, 111.

29. Gay Wilson Allen, "The Poet Must Be Engaged," New York *Times Book Review*, January 8, 1961.

Selected Bibliography

PRIMARY SOURCES

Actfive, and Other Poems. New York: Random House, 1948; Toronto: Random House, 1948; London: John Lane, The Bodley Head, 1948.

Air Raid; a Verse Play for Radio. New York: Harcourt Brace, 1938; London: John Lane, The Bodley Head, 1939; Toronto: George J. McLeod, 1939; New York: Dramatists Play Service, 1939.

America Was Promises (poem). New York: Duell, Sloan and Pearce, 1939; London: John Lane, The Bodley Head, 1940.

The American Cause (prose). New York: Duell, Sloan and Pearce, 1941.

The American Experience (prose). The Hispanic Foundation in the Library of Congress, Washington: Government Printing Office, 1939.

American Opinion and the War. (The Rede Lecture delivered before the University of Cambridge, 30 July, 1942.) Cambridge: The Clarendon Press, 1942; New York: Macmillan, 1942; Toronto: Macmillan, 1942.

The American Story; Ten Radio Scripts. New York: Duell, Sloan and Pearce, 1944, 1960; Toronto: William Collins Sons, 1944; Toronto: Longmans, Green, 1960; Trans., "Los Comuneros," Bogotá, 1945.

Art Education and the Creative Process. New York: Published for the Committee on Art Education by the Museum of Modern Art, 1954.

Background of War. By the editors of *Fortune.* (All but one of the articles are by Archibald MacLeish.) New York: Alfred A. Knopf, 1937.

Before March (poems). Illustrated by Leja Gorska. Borzoi Chapbooks, Number Three. New York: Alfred A. Knopf, 1932.

Collected Poems 1917-1952. Boston: Houghton Mifflin, 1952.

Conquistador (poem). Boston: Houghton Mifflin, 1932; London: Gollancz, 1933; London: Boriswood, 1935; *Dal Poema Conquistador,* a cura di Roberto Sanesi. (English with Italian translation) Varese: Editrice Magenta, 1957.

Einstein (poem). Paris: Black Sun Press, 1929 (limited edition and also limited signed edition).

The Fall of the City; a Verse Play for Radio. New York: Farrar and Rinehart, 1937; London: Boriswood, 1937.

The Free Company Presents; a Collection of Plays about the Meaning of America. New York, 1941.

Freedom is the Right to Choose; an Inquiry into the Battle for the American Future. Boston: Beacon Press, 1951; London: John Lane, The Bodley Head, 1952; Toronto: S. J. Reginald Saunders, 1952.

Frescoes for Mr. Rockefeller's City (poems). John Day Pamphlets, Number twenty-nine. New York: John Day, 1933; Toronto: McLeod, 1933.

The Hamlet of A. MacLeish (poem). Boston: Houghton Mifflin, 1928; second printing, 1930.

The Happy Marriage and Other Poems. Boston: Houghton Mifflin, 1924.

Housing America. By the editors of *Fortune.* New York: Harcourt Brace and Company, 1932.

Selected Bibliography

The Irresponsibles; a Declaration. New York: Duell, Sloan and Pearce, 1940. Trans., *Los Irresponsables.* Buenos Aires, 1942.

J. B.; a Play in Verse. Boston: Houghton Mifflin, 1957, 1958; London: Secker and Warburg, 1959; London: Allen and Unwin, 1959; New York: Samuel French, 1960; Boston: Houghton Mifflin (Sentry Edition), 1961; *J. B.,* versdrama in twee bedrijven, vertaald door V. E. Vriesland. 's-Gravenhage: Boekencentrum, 1959. (Weding-Toneelbibliotheek, serie 4, deel 1); *Spiel um Job.* Deutsch von E. Hesse. Berlin: Suhrkamp, 1958.

Jews in America. By the editors of *Fortune.* New York: Random House, 1936.

Land of the Free—U. S. A. (a book of photographs illustrated by a poem). New York: Harcourt Brace and Company, 1938; Toronto: George J. McLeod, 1938; London: John Lane, The Bodley Head, 1938.

The Next Harvard (prose). Cambridge: Harvard University Press, 1941; New York: Oxford, 1941.

New Found Land; Fourteen Poems. Paris: Black Sun Press, limited edition, 1930; Boston: Houghton Mifflin, limited edition, 1930.

New York; Four Poems. (Four poems by A. MacLeish with Italian translation by M. Guldacci and 25 illustrations by O. Tamburi.) Milano: All' insegna del pesce d'oro, 1958.

Nobodaddy (a play). Cambridge: Dunster House Bookshop, 1926; also limited edition, the same.

Panic; a Play in Verse. Boston: Houghton Mifflin, 1935; London: Boriswood, 1936.

Poems 1924-1933. Boston: Houghton Mifflin, 1933; London: Boriswood, 1935; new edition, London: John Lane, The Bodley Head, 1935, 1943.

Poetry and Experience (prose). Cambridge: Riverside, 1960, 1961; Boston: Houghton Mifflin, 1961; (Sentry Edition), 1961; Toronto: Thomas Allen, 1961; London: The Bodley Head, 1961.

Poetry and Opinion; the Pisan Cantos of Ezra Pound, a Dialogue on the Role of Poetry. Urbana: The University of Illinois Press, 1950.

The Pot of Earth (verse play). Boston and New York: Houghton Mifflin, 1925.

Prophets of Doom (commencement address delivered at the University of Pennsylvania, June 11, 1941). Philadelphia: University of Pennsylvania Press, 1941.

Public Speech; Poems. New York: Farrar and Rinehart, 1936; also limited autographed edition; Toronto: Oxford, 1936; London: Boriswood, 1936.

Songs for a Summer's Day (a sonnet cycle). New Haven: Yale University Press, 1915.

Songs for Eve (poems). Boston: Houghton Mifflin, 1954.

Streets in the Moon (poems). Boston: Houghton Mifflin, 1926; second edition, 1928; limited edition, Cambridge: Dunster House Bookshop, 1926.

The Trojan Horse; a Play. Boston: Houghton Mifflin, 1952.

This Music Crept by Me upon the Waters (a play). (Poets' Theatre Series.) Cambridge: Harvard University Press, 1953; New York: Oxford, 1954; Toronto: S. J. Reginald Saunders, 1954.

Three Short Plays: The Secret of Freedom; Air Raid; The Fall of the City. New York: Dramatists Play Service, 1961.

A Time to Act (selected addresses). Boston: Houghton Mifflin, 1943; London: Allen and Unwin, 1945.

A Time to Speak (selected prose). Boston: Houghton Mifflin, 1941; London: Allen and Unwin, 1941; London: John Lane, The Bodley Head, 1941.

Tower of Ivory (poems). Foreword by Lawrence Mason. New Haven: Yale University Press, 1917.

Union Pacific (an American folk ballet in one act and four scenes). Libretto by Archibald MacLeish, music by Nicholas Nabokoff, choreography by Leonide Massine. Gerald Goode. *The Book of Ballets*. New York: Crown, 1939.

SECONDARY SOURCES

1. Bibliography

MIZENER, ARTHUR. *A Catalogue of the First Editions of Archibald MacLeish*. New Haven: Yale University Library, 1938.

THURBER, GARRISH. "MacLeish's Published Books," *Library Journal*, LXIV (November, 1939), 864, 866.

2. Articles

There is no biography nor an extended critical study of Archibald MacLeish. The following articles represent a cross section of opinion about his work.

ALLEN, GAY WILSON. "The Poet Must Be Engaged," New York *Times Book Review*, January 8, 1961. A thoughtful, perceptive review of *Poetry and Experience*.

BENÉT, WILLIAM ROSE. "Round about Parnassus," *The Saturday Review of Literature*, X (July 29, 1933), 21. A well-stated answer to the most violent of Communist criticisms.

BLACKMUR, R. P. "A Modern Poet in Eden," *Poetry*, XXVIII (September, 1926), 339-42. A review and evaluation of the play *Nobodaddy*.

BRENNER, RICA. *Poets of Our Time*. New York: Harcourt Brace, 1941. Chapter relating personal history and development of poetic skill; recognition of "intuitive sense" as core of his poetry.

DANGERFIELD, GEORGE. "Archibald MacLeish: An Appreciation," *The Bookman*, LXXII (January, 1931), 493-96. *New Found Land* reviewed in relation to earlier work.

EBERHART, RICHARD. "The Pattern of MacLeish's Poetry," New York *Times Book Review*, November 23, 1952. A poet-critic's observations on another poet's life work.

FRIAR, KIMON. "Poet of Action," *New Republic*, CXXVII (December 15, 1952), 19-20. A summary of the poet's extensive career, his courage "to live as a whole being."

GALANTIÈRE, LEWIS. "Hamlet for Our Time," *The Nation*, CXXVIII (April 17, 1929), 471-72. *The Hamlet of A. MacLeish* as reflecting a poet sensitive to his time.

JONES, LLEWELLYN. "A. MacLeish: A Modern Metaphysicist," *English Journal*, XXIV (June, 1935), 441-51. Detailed analysis of *The Pot of Earth*.

Selected Bibliography

KREYMBORG, ALFRED. "The Moon is Dead," *The Saturday Review of Literature*, X (January 27, 1934), 435. The work of MacLeish related to the development of modern poetry and to some of his major contemporaries.

MACLEISH, ARCHIBALD and KAZAN, ELIA. "The Staging of the Play 'J. B.'," *Esquire*, LI (May, 1959), 144-58. Selection from the notebooks and letters indicating how a play can change during production.

MIZENER, ARTHUR. "The Poetry of Archibald MacLeish," *Sewanee Review*, XLVI (October-December, 1938), 501-19. Poet's continuing search for a more complete consciousness of feeling and an appropriate poetic form.

MORSE, SAMUEL FRENCH. "An Act of Faith," *Poetry*, CXC (December, 1961), 191-94. A review of *Poetry and Experience*.

POORE, CHARLES. "Books of the Times," The New York *Times Book Review*, November 29, 1952. Summary of poet's many-sided career and comment on his range and grasp of technique and ideas.

WALTON, EDA LOU. "Archibald MacLeish," *The Nation*, CXXXVIII (January 10, 1934), 48. Observations on the poetic techniques of MacLeish and characteristics of *The Waste Land* school.

WARREN, ROBERT PENN. "Twelve Poets," *The American Review*, III (March, 1934), 212-18. A New Critic's approach to the early poems.

ZABEL, MORTON D. "The Poet on Capitol Hill," *Partisan Review*, VIII (January, 1941), 2-19 and VIII (March, 1941), 128-45. Review colored by marked preference for personal lyrics over public speech.

Index

73168